America Project Making of, J. G. Holland

Kathrina

Her Life And Mine - in a Poem

America Project Making of, J. G. Holland

Kathrina
Her Life And Mine - in a Poem

ISBN/EAN: 9783744709941

Printed in Europe, USA, Canada, Australia, Japan

Cover: Foto ©Thomas Meinert / pixelio.de

More available books at **www.hansebooks.com**

HER LIFE AND MINE,

IN A POEM.

By J. G. HOLLAND,

Author of "Bitter-Sweet."

FORTIETH EDITION.

NEW YORK:
PUBLISHED BY CHARLES SCRIBNER & CO.
1868.

I DEDICATE

"KATHRINA,"

THE WORK OF MY HAND,

TO

ELIZABETH,

THE WIFE OF MY HEART.

INDEX.

KATHRINA.

A TRIBUTE.

More human, more divine than we —
  In truth, half human, half divine —
Is woman, when good stars agree
  To temper with their beams benign
The hour of her nativity.

The fairest flower the green earth bears,
  Bright with the dew and light of heaven,
Is, of the double life she wears,
  The type, in grace and glory given
By soil and sun in equal shares.

True sister of the Son of Man:
    True sister of the Son of God:
What marvel that she leads the van
    Of those who in the path he trod,
Still bear the cross and wear the ban?

If God be in the sky and sea,
    And live in light and ride the storm,
Then God is God, although He be
    Enshrined within a woman's form;
And claims glad reverence from me.

So, as I worship Him in Christ,
    And in the Forms of Earth and Air,
I worship Him imparadised,
    And throned within her bosom fair
Whom vanity hath not enticed.

O! woman — mother!   Woman — wife! —
    The sweetest names that language knows!
Thy breast, with holy motives rife,
    With holiest affection glows,
Thou queen, thou angel of my life!

Noble and fine in his degree
   Is the best man my heart receives;
And this my heart's supremest plea
   For him: he feels, acts, lives, believes,
And seems, and is, the likest thee.

O men! O brothers! Well I know
   That with her nature in our souls
Is born the elemental woe —
   The brutal impulse that controls,
And drives, or drags, the godlike low.

Ambition, appetite and pride —
   These throng and thrall the hearts of men:
These plat the thorns, and pierce the side
   Of Him who, in our souls again,
Is spit upon, and crucified.

The greed for gain, the thirst for power,
   The lust that blackens while it burns:
Ah! these the whitest souls deflour!
   And one, or all of these by turns,
Rob man of his divinest dower!

    1*

Yet man, who shivers like a straw
  Before Temptation's lightest breeze,
Assumes the master — gives the law
  To her who, on her bended knees,
Resists the black-winged thunder-flaw!

To him who deems her weak and vain,
  And boasts his own exceeding might,
She clings through darkest fortune fain;
  Still loyal, though the ruffian smite;
Still true, though crime his hands distain!

And is this weakness? Is it not
  The strength of God, that loves and bears
Though He be slighted or forgot
  In damning crimes, or driving cares,
And closest clings in darkest lot?

Not many friends my life has made;
  Few have I loved, and few are they
Who in my hand their hearts have laid;
  And these were women. I am gray,
But never have I been betrayed.

These words—this tribute—for the sake
  Of truth to God and womankind!
These—that my heart may cease to ache
  With love and gratitude confined,
And burning from my lips to break!

These—to that sisterhood of grace
  That numbers in its sacred list
My mother, risen to her place;
  My wife, but yester-morning kissed,
And folded in Love's last embrace!

This tribute of a love profound
  As ever moved the heart of man,
To those to whom my life is bound,
  To her in whom my life began,
And her whose love my life hath crowned!

Immortal Love! Thou still hast wings
  To lift me to those radiant fields,
Where Music waits with trembling strings,
  And Verse her happy numbers yields,
And all the soul within me sings.

So from the lovely Pagan dream

   I call no more the Tuneful Nine;

For Woman is my Muse Supreme;

   And she with fire and flight divine,

Shall light and lead me to my theme.

KATHRINA.

PART I.

CHILDHOOD AND YOUTH.

PART I.

CHILDHOOD AND YOUTH.

THOU lovely vale of sweetest stream that flows:
Winding and willow-fringed Connecticut!
Swift to thy fairest scenes my fancy flies,
As I recall the story of a life
Which there began in years of sinless hope,
And merged maturely into hopeless sin.

O! golden dawning of a day of storms,
That fell ere noontide into rayless night!
O! beautiful initial, vermil-flowered,
And bright with cherub-eyes and effigies,
To the black-letter volume of my life!

O! faery gateway, gilt and garlanded,

And shining in the sun, to gloomy groves

Of shadowy cypress, and to sunless streams,

Feeding with bane the deadly nightshade's roots,—

To vexing labyrinths of doubt and fear,

And deep abysses of despair and death!

Back to thy peaceful villages and fields,

My memory, like a weary pilgrim, comes

With scrip and burdon, to repose awhile,—

To pluck a daisy from a lonely grave

Where long ago, in common sepulture,

I laid my mother and my faith in God;

To fix the record of a single day

So memorably wonderful and sweet

Its power of inspiration lingers still,—

So full of her dear presence, so divine

With the melodious breathing of her words,

And the warm radiance of her loving smile,

That tears fall readily as April rain

At its recall; to pass in swift review

The years of adolescence, and the paths

Of glare and gloom through which, by passion led,

I reached the fair possession of my power,
And won the dear possession of my love,
And then — farewell!

                Queen-village of the meads
Fronting the sunrise and in beauty throned,
With jeweled homes around her lifted brow,
And coronal of ancient forest trees —
Northampton sits, and rules her pleasant realm.
There where the saintly Edwards heralded
The terrors of the Lord, and men bowed low
Beneath the menace of his awful words;
And there where Nature, with a thousand tongues
Tender and true, from vale and mountain-top,
And smiling streams, and landscapes piled afar,
Proclaimed a gentler Gospel, I was born.

In an old home, beneath an older elm —
A fount of weeping greenery, that dripped
Its spray of rain and dew upon the roof —
I opened eyes on life; and now return,

Among the visions of my early years,

Two so distinct that all the rest grow dim:

My mother's pale, fond face and tearful eyes,

Bent upon me in Love's absorbing trance,

From the low window where she watched my play;

And, after this, the wondrous elm, that seemed

To my young fancy like an airy bosk,

Poised by a single stem upon the earth,

And thronged by instant marvels.   There in Spring

I heard with joy the cheery blue bird's note;

There sang rejoicing robins after rain;

And there within the emerald twilight, which

Defied the mid-day sun, from bough to bough —

A torch of downy flame — the oriole

Passed to his nest, to feed the censer-fires

Which Love had lit for Airs of Heaven to swing.

There, too, through all the weird September-eves

I heard the harsh, reiterant katydids

Rasp the mysterious silence.   There I watched

The glint of stars, playing at hide-and-seek

Behind the swaying foliage, till drawn

By tender hands to childhood's balmy rest.

My Mother and the elm!   Too soon I learned
That o'er me hung, and o'er the widowed one
Who gave me birth, with broader boughs,
Haunted by sabler wings and sadder sounds,
A darker shadow than the mighty elm!
I caught the secret in the street from those
Who pointed at me as I passed, or paused
To gaze in sighing pity on my play;
From playmates who, forbidden to divulge
The knowledge they possessed, with childish tricks
Of indirection strove in vain to hide
Their awful meaning in unmeaning phrase;
From kisses which were pitiful; from words
Gentler than love's because compassionate;
From deep, unconscious sighs out of the heart
Of her who loved me best, and from her tears
That freest flowed when I was happiest.

From frailest filaments of evidence,
From dark allusions faintly overheard,
From hint and look and sudden change of theme
When I approached, from widely scattered words

Remembered well, and gathered all at length
Into consistent terms, I know not how
I wrought the full conclusion, nor how young.
I only know that when a little child
I learned, though no one told, that he who gave
My life to me in madness took his own —
Took it from fear of want, though he possessed
The finest fortune in the rich old town.

Thenceforth I had a secret which I kept —
Kept by my mother with as close a tongue —
A secret which embittered every cup.
It bred rebellion in me — filled my soul,
Opening to life in innocent delight,
With baleful doubt and harrowing distrust.
Why, if my father was the godly man
His gentle widow vouched with tender tears,
Did He to whom she bowed in daily prayer —
Who loved us, as she told me, with a love
Ineffable for strength and tenderness —
Permit such fate to him, such woe to us?
Ah! many a time, repeating on my knees

The simple language of my evening prayer
Which her dear lips had taught me, came the dark
Perplexing question, stirring in my heart
A sense of guilt, or quenching all my faith.
This, too, I kept a secret.   I had died
Rather than breathe the question in her ears
Who knelt beside me.   I had rather died
Than add a sorrow to the load she bore.

Taught to be true, I played the hypocrite
In truthfulness to her.   I had no God,
Nor penitence, nor loyalty, nor love,
For any being higher than herself.
Jealous of all to whom she gave her hand,
I clung to her with fond idolatry.
I sat with her; where'er she walked, I walked;
I kissed away her tears; I strove to fill,
With strange precocity of manly pride
And more than boyish tenderness, the void
Which death had made.

            I could not fail to see

That ruth for me and sorrow for her loss —
Twin leeches at her heart — were drinking blood
That, from her pallid features, day by day
Sank slowly down, to feed the cruel draught.
Nay, more than this I saw, and sadly worse.
Oft when I watched her and she knew it not,
I marked a quivering horror sweep her face —
A strange, quick thrill of pain — that brought her hand
With sudden pressure to her heart, and forced
To her white lips a swiftly whispered prayer.
I fancied that I read the mystery;
But it was deeper and more terrible
Than I conjectured. Not till darker years
Came the solution.

        Still, we had some days
Of pleasure. Sorrow cannot always brood
Over the shivering forms that drink her warmth,
But springs to meet the morning light, and soars
Into the fresh empyrean, to forget
For one sweet hour the ring of greedy mouths
That surely wait, and cry for her return.

My mother's hand in mine, or mine in hers,
We often left the village far behind,
And walked the meadow-paths to gather flowers,
And watch the plowman as he turned the tilth,
Or tossed his burnished share into the sun
At the long furrow's end, the while we marked
The tipsy bobolink, struggling with the chain
Of tinkling music that perplexed his wings,
And listened to the yellow-breasted lark's
Sweet whistle from the grass.

        Glad in my joy,
My mother smiled amid these scenes and sounds,
And wandered on with gentle step and slow,
While I, in boyish frolic, ran before,
Chasing the butterflies, or in her path
Tossing the gaudy gold of buttercups,
Till sometimes, ere we knew, we stood entranced
Upon the river's marge.

        Ever the spell
Of lapsing water tamed my playful mood,

And I reclined in silent happiness
At the tired feet that rested in the shade.
There through the long, bright mornings we remained,
Watching the noisy ferry-boat that plied
Like a slow shuttle through the sunny warp
Of threaded silver from a thousand brooks,
That took new beauty as it wound away;
Or gazing where at Holyoke's verdant base —
Like a slim hound, stretched at his master's feet —
Lay the long, lazy hamlet, Hockanum;
Or, upward turning, traced the line that climbed
O'er splintered rock and clustered foliage
To the bare mountain-top; then followed down
The scars of fire and storm, or paths of gloom
That marked the curtained gorges, till, at last,
Caught by a wisp of white, belated mist,
Our vision rose to trace its airy flight
Beyond the hight, into the distant blue.

One morning, while we rested there, she told
Of a dear friend upon the other side —
A lady who had loved her — whom she loved —

And then she promised to my eager wish
That soon, across the stream I longed to pass,
I should go with her to the lady's home.

The wished-for day came slowly—came at last—
My birthday morning—rounding to their close
The fourteen summers of my boyhood's life.
The early mists were clinging to the side
Of the dark mountain as we left the town,
Though all the roadside fields were quick with toil.
In rhythmic motion through the dewy grass
The mowers swept, and on the fragrant air
Was borne from far the soft, metallic clash
Of stones upon the steel.

This was the day
" So memorably wonderful and sweet
Its power of inspiration lingers still,—
So full of her dear presence, so divine
With the melodious breathing of her words,
And the warm radiance of her loving smile,
That tears fall readily as April rain

2

At its recall." And with this day there came
The revelation and the genesis
Of a new life. In intellect and heart
I ceased to be a child, and grew a man.
By one long leap I passed the hidden bound
That circumscribed my boyhood, and thenceforth
Abjured all childish pleasure, and took on
The purpose and the burden of my life.

We crossed the river — I, as in a dream;
And when I stood upon the eastern shore,
In the full presence of the mountain pile,
Strange tides of feeling thrilled me, and I wept —
Wept, though I knew not why. I could have knelt
On the white sand, and prayed. Within my soul
Prophetic whispers breathed of coming power
And new possessions. Aspiration swelled
Like a pent stream within a narrow chasm,
That finds nor vent nor overflow, but swirls
And surges and retreats, until it floods
The springs that feed it. All was chaos wild, —
A chaos of fresh passion, undefined,

Deep in whose vortices of mist and fire
A new world waited blindly for its birth.
I had no words for revelation ;—none
For answer, when my mother pressed my hand,
And questioned why it trembled.   I looked up
With tearful eyes, and met her loving smile,
And both of us were silent, and passed on.

We reached at length the pleasant cottage-home
Where dwelt my mother's friend, and, at the gate,
Found her with warmest welcome waiting us.
She kissed my mother's cheek, and then kissed mine,
Which shrank, and mantled with a new-born shame.
They crossed the threshold: I remained without,
Surprised—half-angry—with the burning blush
That still o'erwhelmed my face.

      I looked around
For something to divert my vexing thoughts,
And saw intently gazing in my eyes,
From his long tether in the grass, a lamb—
A lusty, downy, handsome, household pet.
There was a scarlet ribbon on his neck

Which held a silver bell, whose note I heard
First when his eye met mine; for then he sprang
To greet me with a joyous bleat, and fell,
Thrown by the cord that held him.   Pitying him,
I loosed his cruel leashing, with intent,
After a half-hour's frolic, to return
And fasten as I found him; but my hand,
Too careless of its charge, slipped from its hold
With the first bound he made; and with a leap
He cleared the garden wall, and flew away.

Affrighted at my deed and its mischance,
I paused a moment—then with ready feet,
And flush and final impulse, I pursued.

He held the pathway to the mountain woods,
The tinkle of his bell already faint
In the long distance he had placed between
Himself and his pursuer.   On and on,
Climbing the mountain path, he sped away,
I following swiftly, never losing sight
Of the bright scarlet streaming from his neck,

Or hearing of the tinkle of his bell,
Till, wearied both, and panting up the steep,
Our progress slackened to a walk.

       At length
He paused and looked at me, and waited till
My foot had touched the cord he dragged, and then
Bounded away, scaling the shelvy cliffs
That bolder rose along the narrow path.
He had no choice but mount.   I pressed him close,
And rocks and chasms were thick on either side.
So, pausing oft, but ever leaping on
Before my hand could reach him, he advanced.
Not once in all the passage had I paused
To look below, nor had I thought of her
Whom I had left.   Absorbed in the pursuit
I pressed it recklessly, until I grasped
My fleecy prisoner, wound and tied his cord
Around my wrist, and both of us sank down
Upon the mountain summit.

       In a swoon
Of breathless weariness how long I lay

I could not know; but consciousness at last
Came by my brute companion, who, alert
Among the scanty browse, tugged at my wrist,
And brought me startled to my feet.   I saw
In one swift sweep of vision where I stood,—
In presence of what beauty of the earth,
What glory of the sky, what majesty
Of lofty loneliness.   I drew the lamb—
The dear, dumb creature—gently to my side,
And led him out upon the beetling cliff
That fronts the plaided meadows, and knelt down.

When once the shrinking, dizzy spell was gone,
I saw below me, like a jeweled cup,
The valley hollowed to its heaven-kissed lip—
The serrate green against the serrate blue—
Brimming with beauty's essence; palpitant
With a divine elixir—lucent floods
Poured from the golden chalice of the sun,
At which my spirit drank with conscious growth,
And drank again with still expanding scope
Of comprehension and of faculty.

I felt the bud of being in me burst
With full, unfolding petals to a rose,
And fragrant breath that flooded all the scene.
By sudden insight of myself I knew
That I was greater than the scene,—that deep
Within my nature was a wondrous world,
Broader than that I gazed on, and informed
With a diviner beauty,—that the things
I saw were but the types of those I held,
And that above them both, High Priest and King,
I stood supreme, to choose and to combine,
And build from that within me and without
New forms of life, with meaning of my own.
And there alone, upon the mountain-top,   .
Kneeling beside the lamb, I bowed my head
Beneath the chrismal light, and felt my soul
Baptized and set apart to poetry.

The spell of inspiration lingered not;
But ere it passed, I knew my destiny—
The passion and the portion of my life:
Though, with the new-born consciousness of power,

And organizing and creative skill,
There came a sense of poverty—a sense
Of power untrained, of skill without resource,
Of ignorance of Nature and her laws
And language and the learning of the schools.
I could not rise upon my callow wings,
But felt that I must wait until the years
Should give them plumage, and the skill for flight
Be won by trial.   .

                    Then before me rose
The long, long years of study, interposed
Between me and the goal that shone afar;
But with them rose the courage to surmount,
And I was girt for toil.

                    Then, for the first,
My eye and spirit that had drunk the whole
Wide vision, grew discriminate, and traced
The crystal river pouring from the North
Its twinkling tide, and winding down the vale,
Till, doubling in a serpent coil, it paused

Before the chasm that parts the frontal spurs
Of Tom and Holyoke ; then in wreathing light
Sped the swart rocks, and sought the misty South.
Across the meadows—carpet for the gods,
Woven of ripening rye and greening maize
And rosy clover-blooms, and spotted o'er
With the black shadows of the feathery elms—
Northampton rose, half hidden in her trees,
Lifted above the level of the fields,
And noiseless as a picture.

                                    At my feet
The ferry-boat, diminished to a toy,
With automatic diligence conveyed
Its puppet passengers between the shores
That hemmed its enterprise ; and one low barge,
With white, square sail, bore northward languidly
The slow and scanty commerce of the stream.

Eastward, upon another fertile stretch
Of meadow-sward and tilth, embowered in elms,
Lay the twin streets, and sprang the single spire

2*

Of Hadley, where the hunted regicides
Securely lived of old, and strangely died;
And eastward still, upon the last green step
From which the Angel of the Morning Light
Leaps to the meadow-lands, fair Amherst sat,
Capped by her many-windowed colleges;
While from his outpost in the rising North,
Bald with the storms and ruddy with the suns
Of the long eons, stood old Sugarloaf,
Gazing with changeless brow upon a scene,
Changing to fairer beauty evermore.

Save of the river and my pleasant home,
I knew not then the names and history
Borne by these visions; but upon my brain
Their forms were graved in lines indelible
As, on the rocks beneath my feet, the prints
Of life in its first motion.   Later years
Renewed the picture, and its outlines filled
With fair associations,— wrought the past
And living present into fadeless wreaths
That crowned each mound and mount, and town and tower,

The king of teeming memories.   Nor could
I guess with faintest foresight of the life
Which, in the years before me, I should weave
Of mingled threads of pleasure and of pain
Into these scenes, until not one of all
Could meet my eye, or touch my memory,
Without recalling an experience
That drank the sweetest ichor of my veins,
Or crowded them with joy.

                    At length I turned
From the wide survey, and with pleased surprise
Detected, nestling at the mountain's foot,
The cottage I had left ; and, on the lawn,
Two forms of life that flitted to and fro.
I knew that they had missed me ; so I sought
The passage I had climbed, and, with the lamb
Still fastened to my wrist, I hasted down.

Full of the marvels of the hour I sped,
Leaping from rock to rock, or flying swift
The smoother slopes, with arms half wings, and feet

That only guarded the descent, the while
My captive led me captive at his will.
So tense the strain of sinew, so intense
The mood and motion, that before I guessed,
The headlong flight was finished, and I walked,
Jaded and reeking, in the level path
That led the lambkin home.

                My mother saw,
And ran to meet me: then for long, still hours,
Couched in a dim, cool room, I lay and slept.
When I awoke, I found her at my side,
Fanning my face, and ready with her smile
And soothing words to greet me.   Then I told,
With youthful volubility and wild
Extravagance of figure and of phrase,
The morning's exploit.

              First she questioned me ;
But, as I wrought each scene and circumstance
Into consistent form, she drank my words
In eager silence ; and within her eyes
I saw the glow of pride which gravity

And show of deep concern could not disguise.
I read her bosom better than she knew.
I saw that she had made discovery
Of something unsuspected in her child,
And that, by one I loved, and she the best,
The fire that burned within me and the power
That morning called to life, were recognized.

When I had told my story, and had read
With kindling pride my praises in her eyes,
She placed her soft hand on my brow, and said:
" My Paul has climbed the noblest mountain hight
"In all his little world, and gazed on scenes
" As beautiful as rest beneath the sun.
" I trust he will remember all his life
" That to his best achievement, and the spot
"Nearest to heaven his youthful feet have trod,
" He has been guided by a guileless lamb.
" It is an omen which his mother's heart
" Will treasure with her jewels."

                              When the sun

Of the long summer day hung but an hour
Above his setting, and the cool West Wind
Bore from the purpling hills his benison,
The farewell courtesies of love were given,
And we set forth for home.

      Not far we fared—
The river left behind—when, looking back,
I saw the mountain in the searching light
Of the low sun. Surcharged with youthful pride
In my adventure, I can ne'er forget
The disappointment and chagrin which fell
Upon me ; for a change had passed. The steep
Which in the morning sprang to kiss the sun,
Had left the scene ; and in its place I saw
A shrunken pile, whose paths my steps had climbed,
Whose proudest hight my humble feet had trod.
Its grand impossibilities and all
Its store of marvels and of mysteries
Were flown away, and would not be recalled.
The mountain's might had entered into me ;
And, from that fruitful hour, whatever scene

Nature revealed to me, she never caught
My spirit humbled by surprise.   My thought
Built higher mountains than I ever found;
Poured wilder cataracts than I ever saw;
Drove grander storms than ever swept the sky;
Pushed into loftier heavens and lower hells
Than the abysmal reach of light and dark;
And entertained me with diviner feasts
Than ever met the appetite of sense,
And poured me wine of choicer vintages
Than fire the hearts of kings.

                  The frolic-flame
Which in the morning kindled in my veins
Had died away; and at my mother's side
I walked in quiet mood, and gravely spoke
Of the great future.   With a tender quest
My mother probed my secret wish, and heard,
With silence new and strange respectfulness,
The revelation of my plans.   I felt
In her benign attention to my words;
In her suggestions, clothed with gracious phrase

To win my judgment; and in all those shades
Of mien and manner which a mother's love
Inspires so quickly, when the form it nursed
Becomes a staff in its caressing hand,
She had made space for me, and placed her life
In new relations to my own.   I knew
That she who through my span of tender years
Had counseled me, had given me privilege
Within her councils; and the moment came
I learned that in the converse of that hour,
The appetency of maternity
For manhood in its offspring, had laid hold
Of the fresh growth in me, and feasted well
Its gentle passion.

            Ere we reached our home,
The plans for study were matured, and I,
Who, with an aptitude beyond my years,
Had gathered learning's humbler rudiments
From her to whom I owed my earliest words,
Was, when another day should rise, to pass
To rougher teaching, and society

Of the rude youth whose wild and boisterous ways
Had scared my childish life.

                        I nerved my heart
To meet the change ; and all the troubled night
I tossed upon my pillow, filled with fears,
Or fired with hot ambitions ; shrinking oft
With girlish sensitiveness from the lot
My manly heart had chosen ; rising oft
Above my cowardice, well panoplied
By fancy to achieve great victories
O'er those whose fellows I should be.

                                At last,
The dawn looked in upon me, and I rose
To meet its golden coming, and the life
Of golden promise whose wide-open doors
Waited my feet.

                    The lingering morning hours
Seemed days of painful waiting, as they fell
In slowly filling numbers from the tower

Of the old village church; but when, at length,
My eager feet had touched the street, and turned
To climb the goodly eminence where he
In whose profound and stately pages live
His country's annals, ruled his youthful realm,
My heart grew stern and strong ; and nevermore
Did doubt of excellence and mastery
Drag down my soaring courage, or disturb
My purposes and plans.

                        What boots it here
To tell with careful chronicle the life
Of my novitiate ?   Up the graded months
My feet rose slowly, but with steady step,
To tall and stalwart manliness of frame,
And ever rising and expanding reach
Of intellection and the power to call
Forth from the pregnant nothingness of words
The sphered creations of my chosen art.
What boots it to recount my victories
Over my fellows, or to tell how all,
Contemptuous at first, became at length

Confessed inferiors in every strife
When brain or brawn contended? Victories
Were won too easily to bring me pride,
And only bred contempt of the low pitch
And lower purpose of the power which strove
So feebly and so clumsily. When won,
They fed my mother's passion, and she praised;
And her delight was all the boon they brought.
My fierce ambition, ever reaching up
To higher fields and nobler combatants,
Trampled its triumphs underneath its feet;
And in my heart of hearts I pitied her
To whose deep hunger of maternal pride
They bore ambrosial ministry.

In all
These years of doing and development,
My heart was haunted by a bitter pain.
In every scene of pleasure, every hour
That lacked employment, every moment's lull
Of toil or study, its familiar hand
Was raised aloft, to smite me with its pang.

From month to month, from year to year, I saw
That she who bore me, and to whom I owed
The meek and loyal reverence of a child,
Was changing places with me, and that she —
Dependent, trustful and subordinate —
Deferred to me in all things, and in all
Gave me the parent's place and took the child's.
She waited for my coming like a child ;
She ran to meet and greet me like a child ;
She leaned on me for guidance and defense,
And lived in me, and by me, like a child.
If I were absent long beyond my wont,
She yielded to distresses and to tears ;
And when I came, she flew into my arms
With childish impulse of delight, or chid
With weak complainings my delay.

                                        By these,

And by a thousand other childish ways,
I knew disease was busy with her life,
Working distempers in her heart and brain,
And driving her for succor to my strength.

The change was great in her, though slowly wrought,—
Though wrought so slowly that my thought and life
Had been adjusted to it, but for this :—
One dismal night, a trivial accident
Had kept me from my home beyond the hour
At which my promise stood for my return.
Arriving at the garden gate, I paused
To catch a glimpse of the accustomed light,
Through the cold mist that wrapped me, but in vain.
Only one window glimmered through the gloom,
Through whose uncurtained panes I dimly saw
My mother in her chamber.   She was clad
In the white robe of rest; but to and fro
She crossed the light, sometimes with hands pressed close
Upon her brow, sometimes raised up toward heaven,
As if in deprecation or despair;
And through the strident soughing of the elm
I heard her voice, still musical in woe,
Wailing and calling.

                    With a noiseless step
I reached the door, and, with a noiseless key,

Turned back the bolt, and stood within. I could
Have called her to my arms, and quelled her fears
By one dear word, and yet, I spoke it not.
I longed to learn her secret, and to know
In what recess of history or heart
It hid, and wrought her awful malady.

Not long I waited, when I heard her voice
Wail out again in wild, beseeching prayer,—
Her voice so sweet and soulful, that it seemed
As if a listening fiend could not refuse
Such help as in him lay, although her tongue
Should falter to articulate her pain.

I heard her voice—O God! I heard her words!
Not bolts of burning from the vengeful sky
Had scathed or stunned me more. I shook like one
Powerless within the toils of some great sin,
Or some o'ermastering passion; or like one ·
Whose veins turn ice at onset of the plague.
"O God," she said, "my Father and my Friend!
"Spare him to me, and save me from myself!

"O! if thou help me not—if thou forsake—

"This hand which thou hast made, will take the life

"Thou mads't the hand to feed.   I cling to him,

"My son,—my boy.   If danger come to him,

"No one is left to save me from this crime.

"Thou knowest, O! my God, how I have striven

"To quench the awful impulse; how, in vain,

"My prayers have gone before thee, for release

"From the foul demon who would drive my soul

"To crime that leaves no space for penitence!

"O! Father! Father! Hear me when I call!

"Hast thou not made me?   Am I not thy child?

"Why, why this mad, mysterious desire

"To follow him I loved, by the dark door

"Through which he forced his passage to the realm

"That death throws wide to all?   O why must I,

"A poor, weak woman—"

          I could hear no more,

But dropped my dripping cloak, and, with a voice,

Toned to its tenderest cadence, I pronounced

The sweet word, "mother!"

                              Her excess of joy
Burst in a cry, and in a moment's space
I sat within her room, and she, my child,
Was sobbing in my arms.   I spoke no word,
But sat distracted with my tenderness
For her who threw herself upon my heart
In perfect trust, and bitter thoughts of Him
Whose succor, though importunately sought
In piteous pleadings by a gentle saint,
Was grudgingly withheld.   Her closing words:
"O! why must I, a poor, weak woman—" rang
Through every chamber of my tortured soul,
And called to conclave and rebellion all
The black-browed passions thitherto restrained.

Ay, why should she, who only sought for God
Be given to a devil?   Why should she
Who begged for bread be answered with a stone?
Ay, why should she whose soul recoiled from sin
As from a fiend, find in her heart a fiend
To urge the sin she hated?—questions all
The fiends within me answered as they would.

O God! O Father! How I hated thee!
Nay, how within my angry soul I dared
To curse thy sacred name!

                Then other thoughts—
Thoughts of myself and of my destiny—
Succeeded. Who and what was I? A youth,
Doomed by hereditary taint to crime,—
A youth whose every artery and vein
Was doubly charged with suicidal blood.
When the full consciousness of what I was
Possessed my thought, and I gazed down the abyss
God had prepared for me, I shrank aghast;
And there in silence, with an awful oath
I dare not write, I swore my will was mine,
And mine my hand; and that, though all the fiends
That cumber hell and overrun the earth
Should spur the deadly impulse of my blood,
And heaven withhold the aid I would not ask;
Though woes unnumbered should beset my life,
And reason fall, and uttermost despair
Hold me a hopeless prisoner in its glooms,

3

I would resist and conquer, and live out
My complement of years.   My bosom burned
With fierce defiance, and the angry blood
Leaped from my heart, and boomed within my brain
With throbs that stunned me, though each fiery thrill
Was charged with tenderness for her whose head
Was pillowed on its riot.

                              Long I sat—
How long, I know not—but at last the sad,
Hysteric sobs and suspirations ceased,
Or only at wide intervals recurred ;
And then I rose, and to her waiting bed
Led my doomed mother.   With a cheerful voice—
Cheerful as I could summon—and a kiss,
I bade her a good night and pleasant dreams ;
And then, across the hall, I sought my room
Where neither sleep nor dream awaited me,
But only blasphemous, black thoughts, and strife
With God and Destiny.

                         I saw it all:
The lamp that from my mother's window beamed,

Illumined other nights and other storms,
And by its lurid light revealed to me
The secrets of a life.   Her sudden pangs,
Her brooding woes, her terrors when alone,
The strange surrender of her will to mine,
Her hunger for my presence, and her fear
That by some slip of fortune she should lose
Her hold on me, were followed to their home—
To her poor heart, that fluttered every hour
With conscious presence of an enemy
That would not be expelled, and strove to spill
The life it spoiled.

                    From that eventful night
She was not left alone.   I called a friend,
A cheerful lady, whose companionship
Was music, medicine and rest ; and she,
Wanting a home, and with a ready wit
Learning my mother's need and my desire,
Assumed the place of matron in the house ;
And, in return for what we gave to her,
Gave us herself.

My mother's confidence,
By her self-confidence, she quickly won ;
And thus, though sadly burdened at my heart,
I found one burden lifted from my hands.
More liberty of movement and of toil
I needed ; for the time was drawing near
When I should turn my feet toward other halls,
To seek maturer study, and complete
The work of culture faithfully begun.

Into my mother's ear I breathed my plans
With careful words.   The university
Was but a short remove — a morning's walk —
Away from her ; and ever at her wish —
Nay, always when I could — I would return ;
And separation would but sweeten love,
And joy of meeting recompense the pain
Of parting and of absence.

                         She was calm,
And leaning in her thought upon her friend,
Gave her consent.   So, on a summer day,

I kissed her faded cheek, and turned from home
To seek the college halls that I had seen
From boyhood's mount of vision.

       Of the years
Passed there in study — of the rivalries,
The long, stern struggles for pre-eminence,
The triumphs hardly won, but won at last
Beyond all cavil, matters not to tell.
It was my grief that while I gained and grew,
My mother languished momently, and lost,—
A grief that turned to poison in my blood.
The college prayers were mummeries to me,
And with disdainful passion I repelled
All Christian questionings of heart and life,
By old and young.

      I stood, I moved alone.
I sought no favors, took no courtesies
With grateful grace, and nursed my haughty pride.
The men who kneeled and gloomed, and prayed and sang,
Seemed but a brood of dullards, whom contempt

Would honor overmuch.   No tender spot
Was left within my indurated heart,
Save that which moved with ever-melting ruth
For her whose breast had nursed me, and whose love
Had given my life the only happiness
It yet had known.

              With her I kept my pledge
With more than faithful punctuality.
Few weeks passed by in all those busy years
In which I did not walk the way between
The college and my home, and bear to her
Such consolation as my presence gave.
In truth, my form was as familiar grown
To all the rustic dwellers on the road
As I had been a post-boy.

              Little joy
These visits won for me — little beyond
That which I found in bearing joy to her —
For every year marked on her slender frame,
And on her cheeks, and on her failing brain,

Its record of decadence.   I could see
That she was sinking into helplessness,
And that too soon her inoffensive soul,
With all its sweet affections, would go down
To hopeless wreck and darkness.

                              From her friend
I learned that still the burden of her prayer
Was, that she might be saved from one great sin —
The sin of self-destruction.   Every hour
This one petition struggled from her heart,
To reach the ear of heaven ; yet never help
Came down in answer to her cry.

                              The Spring
That ushered in my closing college-year
Came up the valley on her balmy wings,
And Winter fled away, and left no trace,
Save here and there a snowy drift, to show
Where his cold feet had rested in their flight.
But one still night, within the span of sleep,

A shivering winter cloud that wandered late
Shook to the frosty ground its inch of rime.
So, when the morning rose, the earth was white;
And shrubs and trees, and roofs and rocks and walls,
Fulgent with downy crystals, made a world
To which a breath were ruin; and a breath
Wrecked it for me, and, by a few sad words,
Blotted the sunlit splendor from my sight.

As I looked out upon the scene, and mused
Of her to whom I hoped it might impart
Some healthy touch of joy, I heard the beat
Of hoofs upon the trackless blank, and saw
A horseman speeding up the avenue.
I raised my sash (I knew he came for me),
And faltered forth my question. From his breast
He drew a folded slip: dismounting then,
He stooped and pressed the missive in a mass
Of clinging snow, and tossed it to my hand.
I closed the window, burst the frosty seal,
And read: "Your mother cannot long survive:
Come home to her to-day." I did not pause

To break the fast of night, but rushing forth,
I followed close the messenger's return.

It was a morning, such as comes but once
In all the Spring,—so still and beautiful,
So full of promise, so exhilarant
With frost and fire, in earth and air, that life
Had been a brimming joy but for the scene
That waited for my eyes — the scene of death —
From which imagination staggered back,
And every sensibility recoiled.

The smoke from distant sugar-camps rolled up
Through the still ether in columnar coils —
Blue pillars of a bluer dome — and all
The resonant air was full of sounds of Spring.
The sheep were bleating round their empty ricks ·
Horses let loose were calling from afar,
And winning fierce replies; the axman's blows
Fell nimbly at the piles which wintry woods
Had lent to summer stores; while far and faint,
The rhythmic ululations of the hound

3*

On a fresh trail, upon the mountain's side,
Added their strange wild music to the morn.

The beauty and the music caught my sense,
But woke within my sick and sinking heart
No motion of response.   I walked as one
Condemned to dungeon-glooms might walk
Through shouts of mirth and festal pageantry,
Hearing and seeing all, yet over all
Hearing the clank of chains and clash of bars,
And seeing but the reptiles of his cell.

How I arrived at home, without fatigue,
Without a thought of effort—onward borne
By one absorbing and impelling thought—
As one within a minute's mete may slide,
O'er leagues of sunny dreamland in a dream,
By magic or by miracle—I found
No time to question.

          At my mother's door
I stood and listened: soon I heard my name

Pronounced within in spiteful whisperings.
I raised the latch, and met her burning eyes.
She stared a wild, mad stare, then raised herself,
And in weak fury poured upon my head
The vials of her wrath.   I stood like stone,
Without the power to speak, the while she rained
Her maledictions on me, and in words
Fit only for the damned, accused my life
Of crimes my language could not name, and deeds
Which only outcast wretches know.

       At length,
I gained my tongue, and tried to take her hand ;
But with a shriek which cut me like a knife
She shrank from me, and hid her quivering face
Within her pillow.

       Then I turned away,
And sought the room where oft in better days
We both had knelt together at my bed,
And, making fast my door, I threw myself
Prone on the precious couch, and gave to grief
My strong and stormy nature.   All the day

With bursts of passion I bewailed my loss,
Or lay benumbed in feeling and in thought,
Tasting no food, and shutting out my soul
From all approach of human sympathy,
Till the light waned, and through the leafless boughs
Of the old elm I caught the sheen of stars.

Then sleep descended—such a sleep as comes
To uttermost exhaustion,—sleep with dreams
Wild as the waking fantasies of her
Whose screams and incoherent words gave voice
To all their phantom brood. ·

                At length I woke.
The house was still as death; and yet I heard,
Or thought I heard, the touch of crafty feet
Upon the carpet, creeping by my door.
It passed away, away; and then a pause,
Still and presageful as the breathless calm
On which the storm-cloud mounts the pallid West,
Succeeded. I could hear the parlor-clock
Counting the beaded silence, and my bed,

Rustling beneath my breathing and my pulse,
Was sharply crepitant, and gave me pain.

An hour passed by, (it loitered like an age),
And then came hurried words and hasty fall
Of footsteps in the passage.   I could hear
Screams, sobs, and whispered calls and closing doors,
And heavy feet that jarred my bed, and shook
The windows of my room.   I did not stir:
I dared not stir, but lay in deathly dread,
Waiting the dread denouement.   Soon it came.
A man approached my door, and tried the latch;
Then knocked, and called.   I knew the kindly voice
Of the physician, and threw back the bolt.
Then by the light he held before his face
I read the fact of death.

                              I took his arm,
And, as I feebly staggered down the stairs,
He broke to me with lack of useless words
The awful truth. . . . The old familiar tale:
She counterfeited sleep: the nurses both,

Weary with over-watching in their chairs,
Under the cumbrous stillness, slept indeed;
And when she knew it, she escaped; and then
She did the deed to which for many years
She had been predisposed.   Perhaps I knew
The nature of the case: perhaps I knew
My father went that way.   I clutched his arm:
There was no need of words.   .

                                  The parlor door
Stood open, and a throng of silent friends,
Choking with tears, gazed on a silent form
Shrouded in snowy linen.   They made way
For me and my companion.   On my knees
I clasped the precious clay, and pouring forth
My pitying love and tenderness for her,
I gave indignant voice to my complaint
Against the Being who, to all her prayers,
For succor and security, had turned
A deaf, dead ear and a repelling hand.

To what blaspheming utterance I gave
My raving passion, may the God I cursed

Forbid my shrinking memory to recall!
I now remember only that when drawn
By strong, determined hands away from her,
The room was vacant.   Every pitying friend
Had flown my presence and the room, to find
Release of sensibility from words
That roused their superstitious souls to fear
That God would smite me through the blinding smoke
Of my great torment.

                Silence, for the rest!
It was a dream ; and only as a dream
Do I remember it: the coffined form,
The funeral—a concourse of the town—
The trembling prayer for me, the choking sobs,
The long procession, the descending clods,
The slow return, articulated all
With wild, mad words of mine, and gentle speech
Of those who sought to curb or comfort me—
All was a dream, from which I woke at length
With heart as dead as her's who slept.   The heavens
Were brass above me, and the breathing world

Was void and meaningless. When told to pray,
This was the logic of my heart's reply:
If God be Love, not such is he to me
Nor such to mine. If He heard not the voice
Of such a lovely saint as she I mourned,
Mine would but rouse His vengeance.

                  So I closed
With Reason's hand the adamantine doors
Which only Faith unlocks, and shut my soul
Away from God, the warder of a gang
Of passions that in darkness stormed or gloomed;
And with each other fought, or on themselves
Gnawed for the nourishment which I denied.

COMPLAINT.

River, sparkling river, I have fault to find with thee:
River, thou dost never give a word of peace to me!
Dimpling to each touch of sunshine, wimpling to each
    air that blows,
Thou dost make no sweet replying to my sighing for
    repose.

Flowers of mount and meadow, I have fault to find with
    you ;
So the breezes cross and toss you, so your cups are filled
    with dew,
Matters not though sighs give motion to the ocean of your
    breath ;
Matters not though you are filling with the chilling drops
    of death!

Birds of song and beauty, lo! I charge you all with
 blame:—
Though all hapless passions thrill and fill me, you are
 still the same.
I can borrow for my sorrow nothing that avails
From your lonely note, that only speaks of joy that never
 fails.

O! indifference of Nature to the fact of human pain!
Every grief that seeks relief entreats it at her hand in vain;
Not a bird speaks forth its passion, not a river seeks the
 sea,
Nor a flower from wreaths of Summer breathes in sym-
 pathy with me.

O! the rigid rock is frigid, though its bed be summer
 mould,
And the diamond glitters ever in the grasp of changeless
 gold ;
And the laws that bring the seasons swing their cycles as
 they must,
Though the ample road they trample blind the eyes with
 human dust.

Moons will wax in argent glory, though man wane to
    hopeless gloom;
Stars will sparkle in their splendor, though he darkle to
    his doom;
Winds of heaven he calls to fan him ban him with an icy
    chill,
And the shifting crowds of clouds go drifting o'er him as
    they will.

Yet within my inmost spirit I can hear an undertone,
That by law of prime relation holds these voices as its
    own,—
The full tonic whose harmonic grandeurs rise through
    Nature's words,
From the ocean's thundrous rolling to the trolling of the
    birds.

Spirit, O! my spirit! Is it thou art out of tune?
Art thou clinging to December while the earth is in its June?
Hast thou dropped thy part in nature? Hast thou touched
    another key?
Art thou angry that the anthem will not, cannot, wait for
    thee?

Spirit, thou art left alone—alone on waters wild;

For God is gone, and Love is dead, and Nature spurns
    her child.

Thou art drifting in a deluge, waves below and clouds
    above,

And with weary wings come back to thee, thy raven and
    thy dove.

KATHRINA.

PART II.

LOVE.

PART II.

LOVE.

As from a deep, dead sea, by drastic lift
Of pent volcanic fires, the dripping form
Of a new island swells to meet the air,
And, after months of idle basking, feels
The prickly feet of life from countless germs
Creeping along its sides, and reaching up
In fern and flower to the life-giving sun,
So from my grief I rose, and so at length
I felt new life returning: so I felt
The life already wakened stretching forth
To stronger light and purer atmosphere.

But most I longed for human love—the source
(So sadly closed), from which my life had drawn
Its sweetest inspiration and reward.
I could not pray, nor could my spirit win
From sights and sounds of nature the response
It vaguely yearned for.   They assailed my sense
With senseless seeming of the hum and whirl
Of vast machinery, whose motive power
Sought its own ends, or wrought for ministry
To other life than mine.

        I could stand still,
And see the trains sweep by; could hear the roar
Of thundering wheels; could watch the pearly plumes
That floated where they flew ; could catch a glimpse
Of thousand happy faces at the glass;
But felt that all their freighted life and wealth
Were nought to me, and moved toward other souls
In other latitudes.

        A year had flown,
And more, when, on a Sunday morn in June,

I wandered out, to wear away the hours
Of growing restlessness.   The worshipers
Were thronging to the service of the day,
And gave me sidelong stare, or shunned me quite;
As if they knew me for a reprobate,
And feared a taint of death.

                    I took the road
That eastward cleft the town, and sought the bridge
That spanned the river, reaching which I crossed.
Then deep within the stripes of springing corn
I found the shadow of an elm, and lay
Stretched on the downy grass for listless hours,
Dreaming of days gone by, or turning o'er
With careless hand the pages of a book
I had brought with me.

                Tired at length I rose,
And, touched by some light impulse, moved along
The old, familiar road.   I loitered on
In a blind revery, nor marked the while
The furlongs or the time, until the spell
In a full burst of music was dissolved.   .

4

I startled as one startles from a dream,
And saw the church of Hadley, from whose doors,
Open to summer air, the choral hymn
Poured out its measured tides, and rose and fell
Upon the silence in broad cadences,
As from a far, careering sea, the waves
Lift into silver swells the sleeping breasts
Of land-locked bays.

                I heard the sound of flutes
And hoarse, sonorous viols, in accord
With happy human voices,—and one voice—
A woman's or an angel's—that compelled
My feet to swift approach.   A thread of gold,
Through all the web of sound, I followed it
Till, by the stress of some strange sympathy,
And by no act of will, I joined my voice
To that one voice of melody, and sang.

The heart is wiser than the intellect,
And works with swifter hands and surer feet
Toward wise conclusions.   So, without resort

To reason in my heart I knew that she
Who sang had suffered—knew that she had grieved,
Had hungered, struggled, kissed the cheek of death,
And ranged the scale of passions till her soul
Was deep, and wide, and soft with sympathy;—
Nay, more than this: that she had found at last
Peace like a river, on whose waveless tide
She floated while she sang. This was the key
That loosed my prisoned voice, and filled my eyes
With tender tears, and touched to life again
My better nature.

        When the choral closed,
And the last chord in silence lapsed away,
I raised my eyes, and, nodding to the beck
Of the old, slippered sexton, I went in,—
Not, (shall it be confessed?) to find the God
At whose plain altar bowed the rural throng;
But, through a voice, to follow to its source
The influence that moved me.

        I was late;
And many eyes looked up as I advanced

Through the broad aisle, and took a seat that turned
My face to all the faces in the house.
I scanned the simpering girls within the choir,
But found not what I sought; and then my eyes
With rambling inquisition swept the pews,
Pausing at every maiden face in vain.
One head, that crowned a tall and slender form,
Was bowed with reverent grace upon the rail
Before her ; and, although I caught no glimpse
Of her sweet face, I knew such face was there,
And there the voice.

     It was Communion Day.
The simple table underneath the desk
Was draped with linen, on whose snow was spread
The feast of love — the vases filled with wine,
The separated bread and circling cups.
The venerable pastor had come down
From his high pulpit, and assumed the seat
Of presidence, and, with benignant eyes,
Sat smiling on his flock. The deacons all
Rose from their pews — four old, brown-handed men,

With frosty hair—and took the ancient chairs
That flanked the table.   All the house was still.
Save here and there the rustle of a silk
Or folding of a fan; and over all
Brooded the dove of peace.   I had no part
In the fair spectacle, but I could feel
That it was beautiful and sweet as heaven.

When the old pastor rose, with solemn mien,
I looked to see the lady lift her head;
But still she bowed; and then I heard these words:
"The person who unites with us to-day
"Will take her place before me in the aisle,
"To give her answer to our creed, and speak
"The pledges of our covenant."

                                Then first
I saw her face.   With modest grace she rose,
Lifted her hat, and gave it to the hand
Of a companion, and within the aisle
Stood out alone.   My heart beat thick and fast
With vision of her perfect loveliness,

And apprehension of the heroism
That shone within her eyes, and made her act
A Christ-like sacrifice.

                      O! eyes of blue!
O! lily throat and cheeks of faintest rose!
O! brow serene, enthroned in holy thought!
O! soft, brown sweeps of hair! O! shapely grace
Of maidenhood, enrobed in virgin white!
Why, in your rapt unconsciousness of me
And all around you—in the presence-hall
Of God and angels—at the marriage-feast
Of Jesus and his chosen—did my eyes
Profane the hour with other feast than yours?

I heard the "You Believe" of the old creed
Of puritan New England; and I heard
The old "You Promise" of its covenant.
Her bow of reverent assent to all
The knotty dogmas, and her silent pledge
Of faithfulness and fellowship, I saw.
These formularies were the frame of oak—

Gnarled, strongly carved, and swart with age and use—
Which held the lovely picture of my saint,
And showed her saintliness and beauty well.

At close of the recital and response,
The pastor raised the plain, baptismal bowl,
And she, the maiden devotee, advanced
And knelt before him.   Lifting then her eyes
To him and heaven, with look of earnest faith
And perfect consecration, she received
Upon her brow the water from his hand.
The trickling chrism shone on her cheeks like tears,
The while he joined her lovely name with God's:

"KATHRINA, I BAPTIZE THEE IN THE NAME
"OF FATHER, SON, AND HOLY GHOST, AMEN!"

Still kneeling like a saint before a shrine,
She closed her eyes.   Then lifting up toward heaven
His hands, the pastor prayed,—prayed that her soul
Might be forever kept from stain and sin;
That Christ might live in her, and through her life

Shine into other souls; might give her strength
To master all temptation, and to keep
The vows that day assumed; might comfort her
In every sorrow, and, in death's dread hour,
Bear her in hopeful triumph to the rest
Prepared for those who love him.

                                    All this scene
I saw through blinding tears.   The poetry
That like a soft aureola embraced
Within its cope those two contrasted forms;
The eager observation and the hush
That reigned through all the house; the breathless spell
Of sweet solemnity and tender awe
Which held all hearts, when she, The Beautiful,
Received the sign of marriage to The Good,
O'erwhelmed me, and I wept.   Shall I confess
That in the struggle to repress my tears
And hold my swelling heart, I grudged her gift,
And felt that, by the measure she had risen,
She had put space between herself and me,
And quenched my hope?

She stood while courtesy
Of formal Christian welcome was bestowed;
Then straightway sought her seat, as though no eyes
But those of One unseen observed her steps.
I saw her taste the sacramental bread,
And touch the silver chalice to her lips;
And while she thought of Him, The Spotless One
Whose flesh and blood were symboled to her heart,
And worshiped in her thought, I ate and drank
Her virgin beauty—with what guilty sense
Of profanation!

Last, the closing hymn
Gave me her voice again; and this I drank;
Nay, this invaded and pervaded me.
Its subtile search found out the sleeping chords
Of sympathy; and on the bridge of sound
It built between our souls, I crossed, and saw
Into the depths of purity and love—
The full, pathetic power of womanhood—
From which the structure sprang. Just once
I caught her eyes. She blushed with consciousness

4*

Of my strong gaze; but paused not in her hymn
Till she had given to every word the wings
That bore it, like a singing bird, toward heaven.

The benediction fell; and then the throng
Passed slowly out.   I was the last to go.
I saw a man whom I had known, and shrank
Both from his greetings and his questionings.
One thing I learned: that she who thus had joined
This cluster of disciples was not born
And reared among their number: that was plain.
I saw it in her bearing and her dress;
In that unconsciousness of self that comes
Of gentle breeding, and society
Of gentle men and women; in the ease
With which she bore the awkward deference
Of those who spoke with her adown the aisle;
In distant and admiring gaze of men,
And the cold scrutiny of village girls
Who passed for belles.

                           I stood upon the steps —

The last who left the door—and there I found
The lady and her friend. The elder turned,
And with a cordial greeting took my hand,
And rallied me on my forgetfulness.
Her eyes, her smile, her manner and her voice
Touched the quick springs of memory, and I spoke
Her name.

She was my mother's early friend,
Whose face I had not seen in all the years
That had flown over us, since, from her door,
I chased her lamb to where I found—myself.
She spoke with tender words and swimming eyes
Of her I mourned, and questioned me like one
Who felt a mother's anxious interest
In all my cares and plans. Why did I not
In all my maunderings and wanderings
Remember I had friends, and visit them—
Not missing her? Her niece was with her now;
Would live with her, perhaps—("a lovely girl!"—
In whisper); and they both would so much like
To see me at their house! (whisper again:

"Poor child! I fear it is but dull for her,
Here in the country.") Then with sudden thought—
"Kathrina!"

        With a blushing smile she turned,
(She had heard every word), and then her aunt—
Her voluble, dear aunt—presented me
As an old friend—the son of an old friend—
Whose eyes had promised he would visit them,
Although, in her monopoly of speech,
She had quite shut him from the chance to say
So much as that.

            I caught the period
Quick as it dropped, and spoke the happiness
I had in meeting them, and gave the pledge—
No costly thing to give—to end my walks
On pleasant nightfalls at the little house
Under the mountain.

            I had spoken more,
But then the carriage, with its single horse,

For which they waited, rattled to the steps,
And we descended.   To their lofty seats
I helped the pair, and in my own I held
For one sweet moment, hand of all the hands
In the wide world I longed to clasp the most.
A courteous "Good Evening, Sir," was all I won
From its possessor; but her lively aunt
With playful menace shook her fan at me,
And said: "Remember, Paul!" and rode away.

"A worldly woman, Sir!" growled a grum throat.
I turned, and saw the sexton.   *Query:* "which?"
"I mean the aunt." . . . "And what about the niece?"
"Too fine for common people!" (with a shrug).
"I think she is," I said, with quiet voice,
And turned my feet toward home.

A pious girl!
And what could I be to a pious girl?
What could she be to me?   Weak questions, these,
And vain perhaps; but such as young men ask
On slighter spur than mine.

                                        She had bestowed
Her love, her life, her goodly self on heaven,
And had been nobly earnest in her gift.
Before all lovers she had chosen Christ;
Before all idols, God; before all wish
And will of loving man, her heart and hand
Were pledged to duty.   Could she be a wife?
Could she be mine, with such unstinted wealth
Of love, and love's devotion, as I craved?
Would she not leave me for a Sunday School
Before the first moon's wane?   Would she not seek
The cant and snuffle of conventicles
"At early candle-light," and sing her hymns
To driveling boors, and cheat me of her songs?
Would she exhaust herself in "doing good"
After the modern styles—in patching quilts,
And knitting socks, and bearing feeble tracts
To dirty little children—not to speak
Of larger work for missionary folk?
Would there not come a time (O! fateful time!)
When Dorcas and her host would fill my house,
And I by courtesy be held at home

To entertain their twaddle, and to smile,
While in God's name and lovely Charity's
They would consume my substance?   Would she not
Become the stern and stately president
Of some society, or figure in the list
Of slim directresses in spectacles?

So much for questions: then reflections came.
These pious women make more careful wives
Than giddy ones.   They do not run away,
Though, doubtless, husbands live whose hearts would heal,
Broken by such a blow!   The time they give
To worship and to pious offices
Defrauds the mirror mainly; and the gold
That goes for charity goes not for gems.

Besides, these pious and believing wives
Make gentle mothers, who, with self-control
And patient firmness, train their children well—
A fact to be remembered.   But, alas!
They train their husbands too, and undertake
A mission to their souls, so gently pushed,

So tenderly, they may not take offense,
Or punish with rebuff; and yet, dear hearts!
With such persistence, that they reach the raw
Before they know it: so it comes to tears
At last, with comfort in an upper room.
But then—a seal is sacred to them, and a purse
Or pocket-book, though in a dressing-room
With shutters and a key!

               Thus wrapped in thought
And selfish calculation of the claims
Of one my peer, or my superior,
In every personal and moral grace,
I walked along, till, on my consciousness,
Flashed the absurdity of my conceits
And my assumptions, and I laughed outright—
Laughed at myself, so loudly and so long
That I was startled.   Not for many months
Had sound of mirth escaped me; and my voice
Rang strangely in my ears, as if the lips
Of one long dead had spoken.

                        I received
The token of returning healthfulness
With warm self-gratulation.   I had touched
The magic hand that held new life for me:
The cloud was lifted, and the burden gone.
The leaf within my book of fate, that gloomed
With awful records, washed and blotched by tears—
Blown by a woman's breath from finger-tips
That knew not what they did—was folded back;
And all the next white page held but one word,
One word of gold and flame—its title-crown,
That wrought a rosy nimbus for itself;
And that one word was LOVE.

                        The laggard days
My pride or my propriety imposed
Upon desire, before my eyes could see
The object of my new-born passion, passed;
And in the low hours of an afternoon,
Bright with the largess of kingly shower
Whose chariot-wheels still thundered in the East,
Leaving the West aflame, I sought the meads,

And once again, thrilled by fore-tasted joy,
Walked toward the mountain.

While I walked, the rain
Fell like a veil of gauze between my eyes
And the blue wall; and from the precious spot
That held the object of my thought, there sprang
An iridal effulgence, faint at first,
But brightening fast, and leaping to an arch
That spanned the heavens—a miracle of light!

"There's treasure where the rainbow rests," I said.
Would it evade me, as, for years untold,
It had evaded every childish dupe
Whose feet had chased the bright, elusive cheat?
Would it evade me?   Question that arose,
And loomed with darker front and huger form
Than the dark mountain, and more darkly loomed
And higher rose as the long path grew short!
Would it evade me?   Like a passing smile
The rainbow faded from the mountain's face;
And Hope's resplendent iris, which illumed

My question, grew phantasmal, and at length
Evanished, leaving but a doubtful blur.
Would it evade me?   Gods! what wealth or waste
Of precious life awaited the reply!
Was it a coward's shudder that o'erswept
My frame at thought of possible repulse
And possible relapse?

                "Oh! there he comes!"
I heard the mistress of the cottage say
Behind a honeysuckle.   Did I smile?
It was because the fancy crossed me then
That the announcement was like one which rings
Over the polar seas, when, from his perch,
The lookout bruits a long-expected whale!
Then sweeping the piazza from the spot
Where with her niece she sat, she hailed me with:
"So, you are come at last!   How very sad
These men have so much business!   Tell me how
You got away; how soon you must return;
Who suffers by your absence; what the news,
And whether you are well?"

                                    Brisk medicine
These words to me, and timely given.   They broke
The spell of fear, and banished my restraint.
She took my arm, and led me to her niece,
Who greeted me as if some special grace
Of courtesy were due, to make amends
For the familiar badinage her aunt
Had poured upon me.

                                    They had come without—
One with her work, the other with her book—
To taste the freshness of the evening air,
Washed of the hot day's dust by rain; to hear
The robin's hymn of joy; and watch the clouds
That canopied with gold the sinking sun.
The maiden in a pale-blue, muslin robe—
Dyed with forget-me-nots, I fancied then,
And sweet with life in every fold, I knew—
A blush-rose at her throat, and in her hair
A sprig of green and white, was lovelier
Than sky or landscape; and her low words fell
More musically than the robin's hymn.

So, with my back to other scene and sound,
I faced the faces, took the proffered chair
And looked and listened.

"Tell us of yourself,"
Spoke the blunt aunt, with license of her years.
"What are you doing now?"

"Nothing," I said.

"And were you not the boy who was to grow
Into a great, good man, and write fine books,
And have no end of fame?"

The question cut
Deeper than she intended. The hot blush
And stammering answer told her of the hurt,
And tenderly she tried to heal the wound:
"I know that you have suffered; but your hours
Must not be told by tears. The life that goes
In unavailing sorrow goes to waste."

"True," I replied, "but work may not be done
Without a motive. Never worthy man
Worked worthily who was not moved by love.
When she I loved, and she who loved me died,
My motive died; and it can never rise
Till trump of love shall call it from the dust
To resurrection."

           I spoke earnestly,
Without a thought that other ears than hers
Were listening to my words; but when I looked,
I saw the maiden's eyes were dim with tears.
I knew her own experience was touched,
And that her heart made answer to my own
In perfect sympathy.

           To change the drift,
I took her book, and read the title-page:
"So you like poetry," I said.

           "So well my aunt
Finds fault with me."

"You write, perhaps?"

"Not I."

"A happy woman!" I exclaimed; "in truth,
The first I ever found affecting art
Who shunned expression by it.　If a girl
Like painting, she must paint; if poetry,
She must write verses.　Can you tell me why
(For sex marks no distinction in this thing),
Men with a taste for art in finest forms
Cherish the fancy that they may become,
Or are, Art's masters?　You shall see a man
Who never drew a line or struck an arc
Direct an architect, and spoil his work,
Because, forsooth! he likes a tasteful house!
He likes a muffin, but he does not go
Into his kitchen to instruct his cook,—
Nay, that were insult.　He admires fine clothes,
But trusts his tailor.　Only in those arts
Which issue from creative potencies
Does his conceit engage him.　He could learn
The baker's trade, and learn to cut a coat,

But never learn to do that one great deed
Which he essays."

                    "'Tis not a strange mistake—
These people make"—she answered, thoughtfully.
"Art gives them pleasure; and they honor those
Whose heads and hands produce it.   If they see
The length and breadth and beauty of a thought
Embodied by another,—if they hold
The taste, the culture, the capacity,
To measure values in the things of art,
Why cannot they create? Why cannot they
Win to themselves the honor they bestow
On those who feed them ?   Is it very strange
That those who know how sweet the gratitude
Which the true artist stirs, should burn to taste
That gratitude themselves ?"

                    " Not strange, perhaps,"
I said, "and yet, it is a sad mistake;
For countless noble lives have gone to waste
In work which it inspired."

Here spoke the aunt:
"You are a precious pair; and if you know
What you are talking of, you know a deal
More than your elders. By your royal leave,
I will retire; for I can lay the cloth
For kings and queens though I may fail to know
Their lore and language. You can eat, I think;
And hear a tea-bell, though you hear not me."
Thus speaking, in her crisp, good-natured way,
The lady left us.

When she passed the door,
And laughter at her jest had had its way,
I said: "It takes all sorts to make a world."

"How many, think you? Only one, two, three,"
The maiden said. "Here we have all the world
In this one cottage—artist, teacher, taught,
In—not to mar the order of the scale.
For courtesy—yourself, myself, my aunt
You are an artist, so my aunt reports;
But, as an artist, you are nought to her.

ร

And now, to broach a petted theory,

Let me presume too boldly, while I say

She cannot understand you, though I can;

You cannot measure her, though she is wise.

You have not much for her, and that you have

You cannot teach her; but I, knowing her,

Can pick from your creations crumbs of thought

She will find manna.   In the hands of Christ

The five loaves grew, the fishes multiplied;

And he to his disciples gave the feast—

They to the multitude.   Artists are few,

Teachers are thousands, and the world is large.

Artists are nearest God.   Into their souls

He breathes his life, and from their hands it comes

In fair, articulate forms to bless the world;

And yet, these forms may never bless the world

Except its teachers take them in their hands,

And give each man his portion."

                              As she spoke

In earnest eloquence, I could have knelt,

And worshiped her.   Her delicate cheek was flushed,

Her eyes were filled with light, and her closed book
Was pressed against her heart, whose throbbing tide
Thridded her temples.   I was half amused,
Half rapt in admiration; and she saw
That in my eyes at which she blushed and paused.
"Your pardon, Sir," she said.   "It ill becomes
A teacher to instruct an artist."

                              "Nay,
It does become you wondrously," I said
With light but earnest words.   "Pray you go on;
And pardon all that my unconscious eyes
Have done to stop you."

                         "I have little more
That I would care to say: you have my thought,"
She answered; "yet there's very much to say,
And you should say it."

                         "Not I, lady, no:
A poet is not practical like you,
Nor sensible like you.   You can teach him

As well as tamer folk.   In truth, I think
He needs instruction quite as much as they
For whom he writes."

              "That's possible," she said,
With an arch smile.

              "Will you explain yourself?"

"Well—if you wish it—yes:" she made reply.
"And first, my auditor must know that I
Believe in inspiration, though he knows
So much as that already, from my words,—
Believe that God inspires the poet's soul,—
That he gives eyes to see, and ears to hear
What in his realm holds finest ministry
For highest aptitudes and needs of men,
And skill to mould it into forms of art
Which shall present it to the world he serves.
Sometimes the poet writes with fire; with blood
Sometimes; sometimes with blackest ink:
It matters not.   God finds his mighty way

Into his verse. The dimmest window-panes
Let in the morning light, and in that light
Our faces shine with kindled sense of God
And his unwearied goodness; but the glass
Gets little good of it ; nay, it retains
Its chill and grime beyond the power of light
To warm or whiten. E'en the prophet's ass
Had better eyes than he who strode his back,
And, though the prophet bore the word of God,
Did finer reverence. The Psalmist's soul
Was not a fitting place for psalms like his
To dwell in over-long, while waiting words,
If I read rightly. As for the old seers,
Whose eyes God touched with vision of the life
Of the unfolding ages, I must doubt
Whether they comprehended what they saw,
Or knew what they recorded. It remains
For the world's teachers to expound their words;
To probe their mysteries ; and relegate
The truth they hold in blind significance
Into the fair domains of history
And human knowledge. Am I understood?"

"You are," I answered; "and I cannot say
You flatter me.   God takes within his hand
A thing of his contrivance which we call
A poet: then he puts it to his lips,
And speaks his word, and puts it down again—
The instrument not better and not worse
For being handled ;—not improved a whit
In quality, by quality of that
Which it conveys.   Do I report aright?
Or do you prompt me?"

                              "You are very apt,"
She said, "at learning, but a little bald
In statement.   Nathless, be it as you say;
And we shall see how it is possible
That poets need instruction quite as much
As those for whom they write.   What sad, bad men
The brightest geniuses have been!   How weak,
How mean in character! how foul in life!
How feebly have the best of them retained
The wealth of good and beauty which has flowed
In crystal streams from God, the fountain head,

Through them to fertilize the world!   Nay, worse
How many of them have infused the tide
With tincture of their own impurity,
To poison sweetest, unsuspecting lips,
And breed diseases in the finest blood!
And poets not alone, and not the worst;
But painters, sculptors—those whose kingly power
And aptitude for utterance divine
Have made them artists:—how have these contemned
In countless instances the God of Heaven
Who filled them with his fire!   Think you that these
Could compass their achievements of themselves?
Can streams surpass their fountains?"

                          "Nay," I said,
In quick response, "Your argument is good;
But is the artist nothing?   Is he nought
But an apt tool—a mouth-piece for a voice?
You make him but the spigot of a cask
Round which you, teachers, wait with silver cups
To bear away the wine that leaves it dry.
You magnify your office."

"We do all

Wait upon God for every grace and good,"

She then rejoined.   "You take it at first hands,

And we from yours: the multitude from ours.

It may leach through our souls, if our poor wills

Retain it not, and drench the fragrant sand.

And if I magnify my office—well!

'Tis a great office.   What would come of all

The music of the masters, did not we

Wait at their doors, to publish to the world

What God has told them?   They would be as mute

As the dumb Sphynx.   They write a symphony,

An opera, an oratorio,

In language that the teacher understands,

And straight the whole world echoes to its strains.

It shrills and thunders through cathedral glooms

From golden organ-tubes and voiceful choirs;

The halls of art of both the hemispheres

Resound with its divinest melodies;

The street stirs with the impulse, and we hear

The blare of martial trumpets, and the tramp

Of bannered armies swaying to its rhythm;

The hurdy-gurdies and the whistling boys
Adopt the lighter strains, and round and round
A million souls its hovering fancies float,
Like butterflies above a fair parterre,
Till, settling one by one, they sleep at last;
And lo! two petals more on every flower!
And this not all; for though the master die,
The teacher lives forever. On and on,
Through all the generations, he shall preach
The beautiful evangel;—on and on,
Till our poor race has passed the tortuous years
That lie prevening the millennium,
And slid into that broad and open sea,
He shall sail singing still the songs he learned
In the world's youth, and sing them o'er and o'er
To lapping waters, till the thousand leagues
Are overpast, and argosy and crew
Ride at their port."

            " True as to facts," I said;
"And as to prophecies, most credible;
But, as an illustration, false, I think.

     5*

That which the voice and instrument may do
For the composer, types may do for those
Who mint their thoughts in verse.   Music is writ
In language that the people do not read—
Is lame in that—and needs interpreters;
While poetry, e'en in its noblest forms
And boldest flights, speaks their vernacular.
Your aunt can read the book within your hand
As well as you, if she desire, yet finds
Your score all Greek, until you vocalize
Its wealth of hidden meaning.   As for arts
Which meet the eye in picture and in form,
They ask no mediator but the light—
No grace but privilege to shine with naught
Between them and the light.   They are themselves
Expositors of that which they expose,
Or they are nothing.   All the middle-men—
The fools profound—who take it on their tongues
To play the showmen, strutting up and down,
And mouthing of the beauty that they hide,
Are an impertinence."

"You leave no room
For critics," she suggested, with a smile.
"We must not spoil a trade, or starve the wives
And innocent babes it feeds."

"No care for them!"
I made reply. "They do not need much room—
Men of their build—and what they need they take.
The feeble conies burrow in the rocks;
But the trees grow, and we are not aware
Of space encumbered by them."

"Yet the fact
Still stands untouched," she added, thoughtfully,
"That greatest artists speak to fewest souls,
Or speak to them directly. They have need
Of no such ministry as waits the beck
Of the composer; but they need the life,
If not the learning, of the cultured few
Who understand them. If from out my book
I gather that which feeds me, and inspires
A nobler, sweeter beauty in my life,

And give my life to those who cannot win
From the dim text such boon, then have I borne
A blessing from the book, and been its best
Interpreter.   The bread that comes from heaven
Needs finest breaking.   Some there doubtless are—
Some ready souls—that take the morsel pure
Divided to their need; but multitudes
Must have it in admixtures, menstruums,
And forms that human hands or human life
Have moulded.   Though the multitudes may find
Something to stir and lift their sluggish souls
In sight of great cathedrals, or in view
Of noble pictures, yet they see not all,
And not the best.   That which they do not see
Must enter higher souls, and there, by art
Or life, be fashioned to their want."

                         "Your thought
Grows subtle," I responded, "and I grant
Its force and beauty.   If the round truth lie
Somewhere between us, and I see the face
It turns to me in stronger light than you

Reveal its opposite, why, let the fault be mine·
It is not yours.   You have instructed me,
And won my thanks."

                    "Instructed you?" she said,
With a fine blush: "you mock, you humble me.
And have I talked so much, with such an air,
That, either earnestly or in a jest,
You can say this to me?"

                        " 'Tis not a sin,
In latitude of ours," I made reply,
" To talk philosophy; 'tis only rare
For beardless lips to do so.   I have caught
From yours a finer, more suggestive scheme
Than all the wise have taught me by their books,
Or by their voices.   I will think of it."

"Now may you be forgiven!" the aunt exclaimed,
Approaching unobserved.   "There never lived
A quieter, more plainly speaking girl,
Than my Kathrina.   All these weeks and months,

I have heard nought from her but common sense;
But when you came, why, off she went; though where
It's more than I know.   You, sir, have the blame;
And you must lift your spell, and give her back
Just as you found her."

        " She has practiced well
Her scheme on us.   She breaks to you the bread
That meets your want; to me, that meets my own,"
I said, in answering.

        "Well," spoke the aunt,
"I think I'll try my hand at breaking bread:
So, follow me."

        We followed to her board,
And there, in converse suited to the hour
And presence of our hostess, proved ourselves—
Quite to that lady's liking—of the earth.
We ate her jumbles for her, sipped her tea,
And reveled in the spicy succulence
Of her preserves.

While still I sat at ease,
The maiden's eye, with quick, uneasy glance,
Sought the clock's dial.   Then she turned to me,
And said with sweet, respectful courtesy:
"Pray you excuse my presence for an hour.
A duty calls me out; and that performed,
I will return."

I saw she marked my look
Of disappointment—that it staggered her—
The while with words of stiffest commonplace
I gave assent.   But she was on her feet;
And soon I heard her light step on the stair,
Seeking her chamber.

"Whither will she go
At such an hour as this, from you and me?"
I coldly questioned of the keen-eyed aunt.

"You men are very curious," she said.
"I knew you'd ask me.   Can't a lady stir,

But you must call her to account?   Who knows
She may not have some rustic lover here
With whom she keeps her tryst?   'Tis an old trick,
Not wholly out of fashion in these parts.
What matters it?   She orders her own ways,
And has discretion."

                              With lugubrious voice
I said: "You trifle, madam, with my wish.
I know the lady has no lover here,
And so do you."

                         "I'm not so sure of that!"
My hostess made response; and then she laughed
A rippling, rollicking roulade, and shook
Her finger at me, till my temples burned
With the hot shame she summoned.

                              "There!" I said;
" You've done your worst, and learned so much, at least—
That I admire your niece.   _I_ curious!
Well, you are curious and cunning too.

Now, in the moment of your victory,
Be generous ; and tell me what may call
The lady from us."

                  " It is Thursday night,"
She answered soberly,—" the weekly hour
At which our quiet neighborhood convenes
For social worship.   You may guess the rest
Without my telling ; but you cannot know
With what anticipated joy she leaves
Our company, or with what shining face
She will return."

                At that, I heard her dress
Sliding the flight, and rising, made my way
To meet her at its foot.   A happy smile
Illumed her features, as she gave her hand
With thought of parting.   I had rallied all
My self-control and gallantry meanwhile,
And said :   " Not here.   I'll with you, by your leave,
So far as you may walk."

                              There was a flash
Of gladness in her eyes, and in her thanks
A subtler charm than gratitude.

                              I bade
My hostess a "good-night," and left her door,
Declining her entreaty to return.
We walked in silence, side by side, a space,
And then, with feigned indifference, I spoke:
" Your aunt has told me of your errand ; else,
It had been modest in me to withhold
This tendance on your steps.   She tells me you
Are quite a devotee.   Whom do you meet,
In neighborhood like this, to give a zest
To hour like this?"

                              " Brothers and sisters all,"
She said in low reply ; "and as for zest,
There's never lack of it where there is love.
When families convene, they have no need
Of more than love to give them festal joy ;

Nor do they with discrimination judge
Between the high and humble.   These are one;
Love makes them one."

            "And you are one with these?"

" Though most unworthy of such fellowship,
I trust that I am one with these;—that they
Are one with me, and reckon me among
Their number."

            "Can they do you any good?"

" They can," she said, "but were it otherwise,
I can serve them; and so should seek them still.
I help them in their songs."

            We reached too soon
The open doorway of the humble hut
Which, for long years, had held the village school,
And, at a little distance, paused.   The room,
Battered and black by wantonest abuse

Of the rude youth, was lit by feeble lamps,
Brought by the villagers ; and scattered round
Upon the high, hacked benches, hardly less
Rude and rough-worn than they, the worshipers
In silence sat.   It was no place for words.
I took the lady's hand, and said "good-night!"
In whisper.   Then she turned, and disappeared
Within the sheltered gloom ; but I could see
The care-worn cheeks light up with pleasant fire
As she passed in ; and e'en the fainting lamps
Flared with new life, the while they caught the breath
Of her sweet robe.   Then with an angry heart
I turned away, and, wrapped in selfish thought,
Took up the walk toward home.

                              This homely group
Of Yankee lollards she preferred to me!
These poor, pinched boobies, with their silly wives—
Ah! these were they who gave her overmuch
In the bestowal of their fellowship!
These crowned her with a peerless privilege,
Permitting her to sit with them an hour

As a dear sister!   How my sore self-love
Burned with the hot affront!

               With lips compressed,
Or blurting forth their anger and disgust,
I strode the meadows, stalked the silent town,
And growled and groaned in sullen helplessness
About the streets, until the midnight bell
Tolled from the old church tower;—in helplessness,
For, mattered nothing what or who she was,
(I had not dared or cared to question that),
Or how offensive in her piety
And her devotion to the tasteless cult
Of the weak throng, I was her slave; and she—
Her own and God's.   The miserable strife
Between my love of self and love of her
I knew was bootless; and the trenchant truth
Cut to the quick.   She held within her hand
My heart, my life, my doom, yet knew it not;
And had she known, her soul was under vows
Which would forever make subordinate
Their recognized possession.

                               But the morn
Brought with it better mood and calmer thoughts.
I had the grace to gauge the heartlessness
Of my exactions, and the power to crush
The tyrant wish to tear her from the throne
To which she clung.   I said: "So she love me
As a true woman loves, and give herself—
Her sweet, pure self—to me, and fill my home
With her dear presence, loyal still to me
In wifely love and wifely offices,
Though she abide in Christian loyalty
By Christian vows, she shall have liberty,
And hold it as her right."

                               She was my peer:
No weakling girl, who would surrender will
And life and reason, with her loving heart,
To her possessor;—no soft, clinging thing
Who would find breath alone within the arms
Of a strong master, and obediently
Wait on his whims in slavish carefulness;—
No fawning, cringing spaniel, to attend

His royal pleasure, and account herself
Rewarded by his pats and pretty words,
But a round woman, who, with insight keen,
Had wrought a scheme of life, and measured well
Her womanhood; had spread before her feet
A fine philosophy to guide her steps ;
Had won a faith to which her life was brought
In strict adjustment—brain and heart meanwhile
Working in conscious harmony and rhythm
With the great scheme of God's great universe,
On toward her being's end.

                    I could but know
Her motives were superior to mine.
I could but feel that in her loyalty
To God and duty, she condemned my life.
Into her woman's heart, thrown open wide
In holy charity, she had drawn all
Of human kind, and found no humblest soul
Too humble for her entertainment, — none
So weak it could return no grateful boon
For what she gave ; and standing modestly

Within her scheme, with meekest reverence ˙
She bowed to those above her, yet with strong
And hearty confidence assumed a place
In service of the world, as minister
Ordained of heaven to break to it the bread
She took from other hands.   And she was one
Who could see all there was of good in me,—
Could measure well the product of my power,
And give it impulse and direction: nay,
Could supplement my power; and help my heart
Against its foes.

     The moment that I thrust
The selfish thirsting for monopoly
Of her affections from my godless heart,
She entered in, and reigned a goddess there.
If she had fascinated me before,
And fired my heart with passion, now she bent
My spirit to profound respect.   I bowed
To the fair graces of her character,
Her queenly gifts, and the beneficence

Of her devoted life, with humbled heart
And self-depreciation.   All of God
That the world held for me, I found in her ;
And in her, all the God I sought.   She was
My saviour from myself and from my sins ;
For, with my worship of the excellence
Which she embodied, came the purity
And peace to which, through all my troubled life,
I had been stranger.   Thoughts and feelings all
Were sublimated by the subtle flame
Which warmed and wrapped me ; and I walked as one
Might walk on air, with things of earth beneath,
Breathing a rare, supernal atmosphere
Which every sense and faculty informed
With light and life divine.

What need to tell
Of the succeeding summer days, and all
Their deeds and incidents?   They floated by
Like silent sails upon a summer sea,
That, sweeping in from farthest heaven at morn,

6

Traverse the vision, and at evening slide
Out into heaven again, their pennant-flames
The rosy dawns and day-falls.   O'er and o'er,
I walked the path, and crossed the stream, that lay
Between me and the idol of my heart ;
And every day, in every circumstance,
I found her still the same, yet not the same ;
For, every day, some unsuspected grace,
Or some fresh revelation of her wealth
Of character and culture, touched my heart
To new surprise, and overflowed the cup
Whose wine was life to me.

                            Though I could see
That I was not unwelcome ; though I knew
I gave a zest to her sequestered life,
I had built up so high my only hope
On her affection—I had given myself
So wholly to the venture for her hand,
I did not dare to speak of love, or ask
The question which, unasked, held hopefully

My destiny : which answered, might bring doom
Of madness or of death.

Meanwhile, I learned
The lady's history from other lips
Than her's—her aunt's.   Alas! the old, old tale!
She had been bred to luxury ; and all
That wealth could purchase for her, or the friends
Swarmed by its golden glamour could bestow,
She had possessed.   But he who won the wealth,
Reaching for more, slipped from his hight and fell,
Dragging his house to ruin.   Then he died—
Died in disgrace ; and all his thousand friends
Fell off. and left his pampered family,
The while the noisy auctioneer knocked down
His house and household gods, and set adrift
The helpless life thus cruelly bereft.
The mother lived a month: the rest went forth,
Not knowing whither ; but they found among
The poor a shelter for their poverty,—
Kathrina with her aunt.   Thus, in few words,

A tragedy of heart-breaks and of death,
Such as the world abounds with.

                              But this girl,
With her quick instincts and her brave, good heart,
Determined she would live awhile, and learn
What lesson God would teach her.   This she sought,
And, seeking, found, or thought she found.   How well
She learned the lesson—what the lesson was—
Her life, thus far revealed, and waiting still
My feeble record, shall disclose.   Enough,
Just now and here, that out of it she bore
A noble womanhood, accepting all
Her great misfortunes as the discipline
Of a paternal hand, in love prescribed
To lead her to her place, and whiten her
For Christian service.

                              All the summer fled;
And still my neart delayed.   One pleasant eve,
When first the creaking of the crickets told

Of Autumn's opening door, I went with her
To ramble in the fields.   We touched the hem
Of the dark mountain's robe, that falls in folds
Of emerald sward around his feet, and there
Upon its tufted velvet we sat down.
It was my time to speak, but I was dumb;
And silence, painful and portentous, hung
Upon us both.   At length, she turned and said:
"Some days have passed since you were latest here.
Have you been ill?"

               "No, I have been at work,"
I answered,—"at my own delightful work;
The first since first we met.   The record lies
Where I may reach it at a word from you.
Command, and I will read it."

               "I command,"
She said, responding with a laugh.   "Nay, I
Entreat.   I used your word, but this is mine,
And has a better sound from lips of mine.
I am your waiting auditor."

I read:

"Was it the tale of a talking bird?
　　Was it a dream of the night?
　When have I seen it?   Where have I heard
　Of the haps of a dainty craft, that stirred
　　My spirit with affright?

"The shallop stands out from the sheltered bay
　　With a burden of spirits twain,—
　A woman who lifts her sad eyes to pray,
　A tall youth, trolling a roundelay,
　　And before them night, and the main!

"O! Star of The Sea!   They will come to harm:
　　Nor master nor sailor is there!
　The youth clasps the mast with his sinewy arm,
　And laughs!   Does he hold in his bosom a charm
　　That will baffle the sprites of the air?

"O! woe to the delicate ship!   O! woe!
　　For the sun is sunk, and behold!

The trooping phantoms that come and go
In the sky above and the waves below!
    Ho! The wind blows wild and cold.

" The woman is weeping in weak despair;
   ·   The youth still clings to the mast,
With cheeks all aflame, and with eyes that stare
At the phantoms hovering everywhere;
    And the storm-rack rises fast!

" The phantoms close on the flying bark;
    They flutter about her peak;
They sweep in swarms from the outer dark;
But the youth at the mast stands still and stark,
    While they flap his stinging cheek.

" They shiver the bolts that the lightning flings;
    They bellow and roar and hiss;
They splash the deck with their slimy wings —
Monstrous, horrible, ghastly things —
    That climb from the foul abyss.

" No star shines out at the woman's prayer ;
O ! madly distraught is she !
And the bark drives on with her wild despair,
With shrieking fiends in the crowded air,
And fiends on the swarming sea.

" Then out of the water before their sight
A shape loomed bare and black !
So black that the darkness bloomed with white ;
So black that the lightning grew strangely bright ;
And it lay in the shallop's track !

" O ! fierce was the shout of the goblins then !
How the gibber and laugh went round !
The shout and the laugh of a thousand men,
Echoed and answered, and echoed again,
Would have been a feebler sound.

" Straight toward the blackness drove the ship ;
But the youth still clung to the mast :
'I have read,' quoth he, with a proud, cold lip,
'That the devil gets never a man on the hip
Whom he scares not, first or last.'

" Nearer the blackness loomed; and the bark
    Scudded before the breeze;
Nearer the blackness loomed, and hark!
The crash of breakers out of the dark,
    And the shock of plunging seas!

" O! woe! for the woman's wits ran daft
    With the fearful bruit and burst;
She sprang to her feet, and flitting aft,
She plunged in the sea, and the black waves quaffed
    The sweet life they had cursed.

" Light leaped the bark on the mountain-breast
    Of a tenth-wave out to land;
While the sprites of the sea fell off to rest,
And the youth, unharmed, became the guest
    Of the elves of the silent land.

" With banter and buffet they pressed around;
    They tied his strong hands fast;
But he laughed, and said, 'I have read and found
That the devil throws never a man to the ground
    Whom he scares not, first or last.'

    6ᶜ

"Under the charred and ghastly gloom,
  Over the flinty stones,
They led him forth to his terrible doom,
And, plunged in a deep and noisome tomb,
  They sat him among the bones.

"They left him there in the crawling mire:
  They could neither maim nor kill:
For fiends of water, and earth, and fire,
Are baffled and beaten by the ire
  Of a dauntless human will.

" Days flushed and faded, months passed away,
  He knew by the golden light
That shot, through a loop in the wall, the ray
Which parted the short and slender day
  From the long and doleful night.

"Was it a vision that cheated his eyes?
  Was he awake, or no?
He stared through the loop with keen surprise;
For he saw a sweet angel from the skies,
  With white wings, folded low.

"Could she not loose him from his thrall,
    And lead him into the light?
'Ah me!' he murmured, 'I dare not call,
Lest she may doubt it a goblin's waul,
    And leave me in swift affright!'

"She plumed her wings with a noiseless haste;
    He could neither call nor cry:
She vanished into the sunny waste,
Into far blue air that he longed to taste;
    And he cursed that he could not die.

"But she came again, and every day
    He worshiped her where she shone;
And again she left him and floated away,
But his faithless tongue refused to pray
    For the boon she could give alone.

"And there he sits in his dumb despair,
    And his watching eyes grow dim:
Would God that his coward lips might dare
To utter the word to the angel fair,
    That is life or death to him!"

I marked her as I read, a furtive glance
Filling each pause.   The passion of the piece,
Flaming and fading, ever and anon,
Mirrored itself within her tender eyes,
Themselves the mirror of her tender soul,
And fixed attent upon my face the while.

She had not caught my meaning, but had heard
Only a weird, wild story.   When I paused,
Folding the manuscript, I saw a shade
Of disappointment sweep her face, and marked
A question rising in her eyes.   She knew
That I was waiting for her words, and turned
Her look away, and for long moments gazed
Into the brooding dusk.

                 "Speak it!" I said.

" 'Twas very strange and sad," she answered me.
"Why do you write such things?—or, writing such,
Leave them so incomplete?   The prisoned youth,
Thus unreleased, will haunt me while I live.
I shudder while I think of him."

Then I:

"The poem will be finished, by-and-by,
For this is history, and antedates
No fact that it records. Whether this youth
Shall live entombed, or reach the blessed air,
Depends upon his angel ; for he calls—
I hear him call, and call again her name
Kathrina !   O ! Kathrina !"

Like the flash
Of the hot lightning, the significance
Of the strange vision gleamed upon her face
In a bright, throbbing flame, that fell full soon
To ashen paleness.   By unconscious will
We both arose.   She vainly tried to speak,
And gazed into my eyes with such a look
Of tender questioning, of half-reproach,
Of struggling, doubting, hesitating joy,
As few men ever see, and none but once.

Are there not lofty moments, when the soul
Leaps to the front of being, casting off

The robes and clumsy instruments of sense,
And, postured in its immortality,
Reveals its independence of the clod
In which it dwells?—moments in which the earth
And all material things, all sights and sounds,
All signals, ministries, interpreters,
Relapse to nothing, and the interflow
Of thought and feeling, love and life go on
Between two spirits, raised to sympathy
By an inspiring passion, as, in heaven,
The body dust, within an orb outlived,
It shall go on forever?

                    Moments like these—
Nay, these in very truth—were given us then.
Who shall expound—ah! who but God alone,
The everlasting mystery of love?
She spoke not, but I knew that she was mine.
I breathed no word, but she was well assured
That I was wholly her's.   .

                    In what disguise

Our love had hid, and wrought its miracle;
Behind what semblance of indifference,
Or play of courtesy, it spun the cords
That bound our hearts in one, was mystery
Like love itself. The swift intelligence
Of interchange of perfect faith and troth,
Of gift of life and person, of the thrill
Of triumph in my soul and gratitude
In hers, without a gesture, or a word,
Was like the converse of the continents—
Tracking with voiceless flight the slender wire
That underlay the throbbing mystery
Between our souls, and made our heart-beats one.
I opened wide my arms, and she, my own,
Sobbed on my breast with such excess of joy,
In such embrace of passionate tenderness,
As heaven may yield again, but never earth.

Slow in the golden twilight, toward her home,
Her hand upon my arm, we loitered on,
Silent at first, and then with quiet speech
Broaching our plans, or tracing in review

The history of our springing love, when she,
Lifting her soft blue eyes to mine:

                    " Dear Paul!
There are some things, and some I will not name,
That make me sad, e'en in this hight of joy.
In the wild lay that you have read to-night,
You make too much of me.   No heart of man,
Though loving well and loving worthily,
Can be content with any human love.
No woman, though the pride and paragon
Of all her sex, can take the place of God.
No angel she : nor is she quite a man
In power and courage,—gifts which charm her most,
And which, possessing most, disrobe her charms,
And make her less a woman.   If she stand
In fair equality with man—his mate—
Each unto each the rounded complement
Of their humanity, it is enough ;
And such equality must ever lie
In their unequal gifts.   This thing, at least,
Is true as God: she is not more than he,

And sits upon no throne.   To be adored
By man, she must be placed upon a throne
Built by his hands, and sit an idol there,
Degraded by the measure of the flight
Between God's thought and man's."

Responding, I :
" Fix your own place, my love ; it is your right.
'Tis well to have a theory, and sit
In the centre of it, mistress of its law,
And subject also ;—to set men up here
And women there, in a fine equipoise
Of gift and grace and import.   It conveys
To nicely-working minds a pleasant sense
Of order, like a well-appointed room,
Where one may see, in various stuffs and wares,
Forethoughts of color brought to harmony ;
Strict balancings of quantity and form ;
Flowers in the center, and, beside the grate,
A rack for shovel and tongs.   But minds like these
(Your pardon, love !) are likely to arrange
The window-lights to save the furniture,

And spoil the pictures on the wall.   And you,
In the adjustment of your theory,
Would shut the light from her whose mind informs
Its harmonies.   All worship, in my thought,
Goes hand in hand with love.   We cannot love,
And fail to worship what we love.   While you
Worship the strength and courage which you find
In him who has your heart, he'bows to all
Of faith and sweetness which he finds in you.
If, in our worship, we have need to build
Noblest ideals, taking much from God
With which to make them perfect in our eyes,
Shall God mark blame?   We worship him the while,
In attributes his own, or attributes
With which our thought invests him.   As for me—
It is no secret—I am what you call
A godless man ; yet what is worshipful,
Or seems to be so, that with all my heart
I worship ; and I worship while I love.
You deem yourself the dwelling-place of God,
And keep your spirit cleanly for his feet.
All merit you abjure, ascribing all

To him who dwells within you.   How can you
Forbid that I fall down and worship you,
When what I find to worship is not yours,
But God's alone?   I know the ecstasy
Enlarges, strengthens, purifies my soul,
And blesses me with peace.   My love, my life,
You are my all.   I have no other good,
And, in this moment of my happiness,
I ask no other."

                  Tears were in her eyes,
Her clasped hands clinging fondly to my arm,
While under droop of lashes she replied :
" I feel, dear Paul, that this is sophistry.
It does not touch my judgment or my heart
With motive of conviction.   In what way
God may be working to reclaim your will
And worship to himself, I cannot know.
If through your love for me, or mine for you,
Then, as his grateful, willing instrument,
I yield myself to him.   But this is true:
God is not worshiped in his attributes.

I do not love your attributes, but you.
Your attributes all meet me otherwhere,
Blended in other personalities,
Nor do I love, nor do I worship them,
Or those who bear them.   E'en the spotted pard
Will dare a danger which will make you pale,
But shall his courage steal my heart from you?
You cheat your conscience, for you know that I
May like your attributes, yet love not you ;
Nay, worship them indeed, despising you.
I do not argue this to damp your joy,
But make it rational.   If you presume
Perfection in me,—if you lavish all
The largess of your worship and your love
On me, imposing on my head a crown
Stolen from God's, there surely waits your heart
The pang of disappointment.   There will come
A sad, sad time, when, in your famished soul,
The cry for something more, and more divine,
Will rise, nor be repressed."

                              There is a charm

In earnestness, when it inspires the lips
Of one we love, that spoils their argument,
And yields so much of pleasure and of pride,
That the conviction which they seek evades
Their eager fingers, and with throbbing wings.
Crows from its covert.

                She was casuist,
Cunning and clear ; and I was proud of her ;
And though I knew that she had swept away
My refuges of lies like chaff, and proved
My fair words fustian, I was moved to mirth
Over the solemn ruin. Had it been
A decent thing to do, I should have laughed
Full in her face ; but knowing that her words
Were offspring of her conscience and her love,
I could no less than hold respectfully
Her earnest warning.

           "Well, I'll take the risk,"
I said. "While you shall have the argument,
I will have you, who, on the whole, I like

Better than that.   And you shall have your way,
And I my own, in common liberty,
With things like these.   You, doubtless, are to me
What I am not to you.   We are unlike
In life and circumstance — alike alone
In this: that better than all else on earth
We love each other.   This is basis broad
For happiness, or broad enough for me.
If you build better, you are fortunate,
Ay, fortunate indeed; and some fine day
We'll talk about it.   Let us have to-night
Joy in our new possessions, and defer
This little joust of wits and consciences
To more convenient season."

                              We had reached
The cottage door at this; and there her aunt
Awaited our return.   So, hand in hand,
Assuming show of rustic bashfulness,
We paused before her, and with bows profound
Made our obeisance.

"Well?" she said at length;
"Well?—and what of it?"

"Are you not surprised?"
I asked.

"Surprised, indeed! Surprised at what?"

"At what you see: and this! and this!" I said,
Planting a kiss upon each lovely cheek
Of my betrothed, that straightway bloomed with rose.
"What! are you blind, my aunt?"

"You silly fools!
I've seen it from the first," she answered me.
"No doubt you thought that you were very deep,
Very mysterious—all that sort of thing.
I've watched you, and if you, young man, had been
Aught but a coward, it had come before,
And saved some sleep o'nights to both of you.
But down upon your knees, for benison
Of one who loves you both."

                                   We knelt, and then
She kissed us, leaving on our cheeks the tears
That sprang to brim the moment.   Her shrewd eyes,
That melted in the sympathy of love,
Would not meet ours again, but turned away,
And sought in solitude to drain themselves
Of their strange passion.

                                   God forbid that I,
With weak and sacrilegious lips, betray
The confidence of love ; or tear aside
The secresy behind whose snowy folds
Honor and virgin modesty retire
For holiest communion !   For the fire
Which burns upon that altar is of God.
Its tongues of flame, throughout all time and space,
Speak but one language, understood by all,
But sacred ever to the wedded hearts
That listen to their breathings.

                                   And for him,
The poet-pimp, the vile, salacious knave,

Who prostitutes his love, his verse, himself,

And those who drink the poison of his ink,

By revelations of the mystery

That wraps this double being, reveling

In the base element which love alone

As pure as God can wholly purify,

While it repeats the miracle of life

Through all the generations ;—for the man

Who makes a lover brother of the beast,

And her whom he dishonors by his love,

His fitting consort ; who adorns the filth

He digs from styes with wreaths of poesy,

And with his smutted hand presents the dish

For the world's eating, claiming for himself

The poet's crown — ay, winning it from those

Who share his beastliness ;—for him, I say,

The imprecations of all womankind,

With man's "Amen!"

                    In the deep hours of night

I left the cottage, brain and heart o'erfilled

7

With the ethereal vintage I had quaffed.
Disturbing not the drowsy ferryman,
I slipped his little wherry from the sand,
And in the star-sprent river lipped the oars
That pulled me homeward.   The enchanting tide
Was smooth continuation of the dream
On which my spirit, holily afloat,
Had glided through long hours of happiness.
Earth, by the strange, delicious ecstasy,
Was changed to paradise ; and something kin
To gratitude arose within my soul—
A fleeting passion, dying all too soon,
Lacking the root which faith alone can feed.

I touched the shore ; but when my hasting feet
Started the homeward walk, there came a change.
Down from the quiet stars there fell a voice,
Heard in the innermost, that troubled me :
"She is not more than you : why worship her ?
"And she will die : what will remain for you ?
"You may die first, indeed : then what resource ?
"You have no sympathy with her in things

"Ordained within her conscience and her life
" The things supreme: can there be marriage thus?
" Is e'en such bliss as may be possible
" Sure to be yours?   Fate has a thousand hands
" To dash your lifted cup."

    With thoughts like these,
A vague uneasiness invaded me,
And toned the triumph of my passion, till,
Almost in anger, I exclaimed at last:
" This is reaction.   I have flown too high
" Above the healthy level, and I feel
" The press of denser air.   The equipoise
" Of circumstance and feeling will be reached
" All in good time.   Rest and to-morrow's sun
" Will bring the remedy, and, with the mists,
" This cloud will pass away."

    Then with clenched hands
I swore I would be happy,—that my soul
Should find its satisfaction in her love ;
And that, if there should ever come a time

Of cold satiety, or I should find

Weakness or fault where I had thought was strength

And full perfection, I would e'en endow

Her poverty with all the hoarded wealth

Of my imagination, making her

The woman of my want, in plenitude

Of strength and loveliness.

                                         The breezy days

Over whose waves my buoyant life careered,

Rolled to October, falling on its beach

With bursts of mellow music ; and I leaped

Upon the longed-for shore ; for, in that month,

My dear betrothed, deferring to the stress

Of my impatient wish, had promised me

Her hand in wedlock.

                                         Ere the happy day

Dawned on the world, the world was draped in robes

Meet for the nuptials.   Baths of sunny haze,

Steeping the ripened leaves from day to day,

And dainty kisses of the frost at night,
Joined in the subtile alchemy that wrought
Such miracles of change, that myriad trees
Which pranked the meads and clothed the forest glooms
Bloomed with the tints of Eden.   Had the earth
Been splashed with blood of grapes from every clime,
Tinted from topaz to dim carbuncle,
Or orient ruby, it would not have been
Drenched with such waste of color.   All the hues
The rainbow knows, and all that meet the eye
In flowers of field and garden, joined to tell
Each tree's close-folded secret.   Side by side
Rose sister maples, some in amber gold,
Others incarnadine or tipped with flame ;
And oaks that for a hundred years had stood,
And flouted one another through the storms—
Boasting their might—proclaimed their pique or pride
In dun, or dyes of Tyre.   The sumac-leaves
Blazed with such scarlet that the crimson fruit
Which hung among their flames was touched to guise
Of dim and dying embers; while the hills
That met the sky at the horizon's rim—

Dabbled with rose among the evergreens,
Or stretching off in sweeps of clouted crimson—glowed
As if the archery of sunset clouds,
By squads and fierce batallions, had rained down
Its barbed and feathered fire, and left it fast
To advertise the exploit.

                    In such pomp
Of autumn glory, by the simplest rites,
Kathrina gave her hand to me, and I
Pledged truth and life to her.   I bore her home
Through shocks of maize, revealing half their gold,
Past gazing harvesters with creaking wains
That brimmed with fruitage—my adored, my wife,
Fruition of my hope—the proudest freight
That ever passed that way!

                    My troops of friends,
Grown strangely warm and strangely numerous
With scent of novelty and pleasant cheer,
Assisted me to place upon her throne
My household queen.   Right royally she sat

The new-born dignity. Most graciously
She spoke and smiled among the silken clouds
That, fold on perfumed fold, like frankincense
Enveloped her, through half the festal night,
With welcome and good wishes. I was proud;
For was not I a king where she was queen?
And queen she was—though consort in my home,
Queen regnant in the realm of womanhood,
By right of every charm.

                  Into her place,
As mistress of all home economies,
She slid without a jar, as if the Fates,
By concert of foreordinate design,
Had fitted her for it, and it for her,
And, having joined them well, were satisfied.
Obedient to the orbit of our love,
We came and went, revolving round our home
In spheral harmony—twin stars made one,
And loyal to one law.

                  When at our board,

All viands lifted by her hand became
Ambrosial ; and her light, elastic step
From room to room, in busy household cares,
Timed with my heart, and filled me with a sense
Of harmony and peace.   Days, weeks and months
Lapsed like soft measures, rhyming each with each,
All charged with thoughtful ministries to me,
And not to me alone ; for I was proud
To know that she was counted by the good
As a good power among them,—by the poor,
As angel sent of God, on whom they called
His blessing down.

                    She held her separate life
Of prayer and Christian service, without show
Of sanctity, without obtrusiveness ;
And, though I could but know she never sought
A blessing for herself, forgetting me
In her petition, not in all those months
Did word of difference betray the gulf
Between our souls and lives.   She had her plan:
I guessed it, and respected it.   She felt

That if her life were not an argument
To move me, nothing that her lips might say
Could win me to her wish. Pride would repel
What it could not refute, and pleasantry
Parry the thrusts that love could not resent.

A whole year sped, yet not a line of verse
Had grown beneath my pen. When I essayed
To brace my powers to effort, and to call
Forth from their camp and covert the bright ranks
Of tuneful numbers, no responsive shout
Answered the bugle-blast, and from my hand —
Irresolute and nerveless as a babe's —
My falchion fell.

She rallied me on this ;
But I had naught to say, save this, perhaps :
That she, being all my world, had left no room
For other occupation than my love.
She did not smile at this: it was no jest,
But saddest truth. I had grown enervate
In the warm atmosphere which I had breathed ;

7*

And this, with consciousness that in her soul—
As warm with love as mine—each gentle power
Was kindling with new life from day to day,
Growing with my decline.

                    Well, in good time,
There came to us a child, the miniature
Of her on whose dear breast my babyhood
Was nursed and cradled ; and my happy heart,
Charged with a double tenderness, received
And blessed the precious gift.   Another fount
Of human love gurgled to meet my lips.
Another store of good, as rich and pure,
In its own kind, as that from which I drank,
Was thus discovered to my taste, and I
Feasted upon its fullness.

                    With the gift
That brimmed my cup of joy, there came a grace
To her who bore it of fresh loveliness.
If I had loved the maiden and the bride,

The mother, through whose pain my heart had won
Its new possession, fastened to my heart
With a new sympathy.   Whatever dross
Our months of intimacy had betrayed
Within her character, was purged away,
And she was left pure gold.   Nay, I should say,
Whatever goodness had not been revealed
Through the relations of her heart to mine
As loving maid and mistress, found the light
Through her maternity.   A heavenly change
Passed o'er her soul and o'er her pallid face,
As if the unconscious yearning of a life
Had found full satisfaction in the birth
Of the new being.   Her long weariness
Was but a trance of peace and gratitude ;
And as she lay — her babe upon her breast,
Her eyelids closed — I could but feel that heaven,
Should it hold all the good of which she dreamed,
Had little more for her.

                    And when again
She moved about the house, in ministry

To me and to her helpless child, I knew
That I had tasted every precious good
That woman bears to man.   Ay, more than this:
That not one man in thousands had received
Such largess of affection, and such prize
Of womanhood, as I had found in her,
And made my own.   The whole enchanting round
Of pure, domestic commerce had been mine.
A lover blest, a husband satisfied,
A father crowned!   Love had no other boon
To offer me, and held within its gift
No other title.

               Thus, within the space
Of two swift years, I traversed the domain
Of novelty, and learned that I must glean
The garnered fields of my experience
To gratify the greed that still possessed
My sateless heart.   The time had come to me—
Which I had half foreseen—when, by my will,
My interest in those I loved should live
Predominant in all my life.   I nursed

With jealous care my passion for my wife.
I raised her to an apotheosis
In my imagination, where I bowed
And paid my constant homage.   I was still
Her fond and loyal lover ; but my heart,
That had so freely drunk, with full content,
Had seen the bottom of the cup she held ;
And what remained but tricks to eke it out,
And artifice to give it piquancy,
And sips to cool my tongue, the while my heart
Was hollow with its thirst?   My little child
Was precious to my soul beyond all price ;
Mother and babe were all that they could be
To any heart of man ; and yet—and yet !

Of all the dull, dead weights man ever bore,
Sure, none can wear the soul with discontent
Like consciousness of power unused.   To feel
That one has gift to move the multitude,—
To act upon the life of humankind

By force of will, or fire of eloquence,
Or voice of lofty art, and yet, to feel
No stir of mighty motive in the soul
To action or endeavor ; to behold
The fairest prizes of this fleeting life
Borne off by patient men who, day by day,
By bravest toil and struggle, reach the hights
Of great achievement, toiling, struggling thus
With a strong joy, and with a fine contempt
For soft and selfish passion ; to see this,
Yet cling to such a passion, like a slave
Who hugs his chains in sluggish impotence,
Refusing freedom lest he lose the crust
The chain of bondage warrants him — ah! this
Is misery indeed !

                    Such misery
Was mine.   I held the consciousness of power
To labor even-headed with the best
Who wrought for fame, or strove to make themselves
Felt in the world's great life ; and yet, I felt
No lift to enterprise, from heaven above

Or earth beneath ; for neither God nor man
Lived in my love.   My home held all my world ;
Yet it was evident — I felt, I knew —
That nought could fill my opening want but toil ;
And there were times when I had hailed with joy
The curse of poverty, compelling me
To labor for my bread, and for the bread
Of those I loved.

          My neighbors all around
Were happy in their work.   The plodding hind
Who served my hand, or groomed my petted horse,
Whistled about his work with merry heart,
And filled his measure of content with toil.
In all the streets and all the busy fields,
Men were astir, and doing with their might
What their hands found to do.   They drove the plough,
They trafficked, builded, delved, they spun and wove,
They taught and preached, they hasted up and down
Each on his little errand, and their eyes
Were full of eager fire, as if the earth
And all its vast concerns were on their hands.

Their homes were fresh with guerdon every night,
And ripe with impulse to new industry
At each new dawn.

               I saw all this, but knew
That they were not like me—were most unlike
In constitution and condition.   Thus,
My power to do, and do the single thing
My power was shaped to do, became, instead
Of wings to bear me, weights to burden me.
The moiling multitude for little tasks
Found little motives plenty; but for me,
Who in my indolence they all despised—
Not understanding me—no motive rose
To lash or lead.   Even the love I dreamed
Would give me impulse had defrauded me.
Feeble and proud ; strong, yet emasculate ;
Centered in self, and still despising self ;
Goaded, yet held ; convinced, but never moved ;
Such conflict ofttimes held and harried me
That death had met with welcome.   If I read,
I read to kill my time.   No interest

In the great thoughts of others moved my soul,
Because I had no object: useless quite
The knowledge and the culture I possessed ;
And if I rode, the stale monotony
Of the familiar landscapes sickened me.

In these dull years, my toddling little wean
Grew into prattling childhood, and I gained
Such fresh delight from her as kept my heart
From fatal gloom ; but more and more I shunned
The world around me, more and more drew in
The circle of my life, until, at last,
My home became my hermitage. I knew
The dissolution of the spell would come,
And, though I dreaded it, I longed to greet
The crash and transformation. If my pride
Forbade the full confession to my wife
That time had verified her prophecy,
It failed to hold the truth from her. She read,
With a true woman's insight, all my heart ;
But with a woman's sensitiveness shrank
From questions which might seem to carry blame ;

And so, for years, there lay between our souls
The bar of silence.

            One sweet summer eve,
After my lamb was folded and before
The lamps were lighted, as I sat alone
Within my room, I heard reluctant feet
Seeking my door.   They paused, and then I heard :

" May I come in ? "

            " Ay, you may always come ;
And you are welcome always," I replied.

The room was dim, but I could see her face
Was pale, and her long lashes wet.   "Your seat"—
I said, with open arms.   Upon my knee,
One hand upon my shoulder, she sank down
As if the heart within her breast were lead,
And she were weary with its weight.

          " My wife,
What burden now ? " I asked her tenderly.

She fixed her swimming eyes on mine, and said:
"My dear, you are not happy. Years have gone
Since you have been content. I bring no words
Of blame against you: you have been to me
A comfort and a joy. Your constancy
Has honored me as few of all my sex
Are honored by your own; but while you pine
With secret pain, I am so wholly yours
That I must pine with you. I've waited long
For you to speak; and now I come to you
To ask you this one question: is there aught
Of toil or sacrifice within my power
To ease your heart, or give you liberty
Beyond the round to which you hold your feet?
Speak freely, frankly, as to one who loves
Her husband better than her only child,
And better than herself."

                    I drew her head
Down to my cheek, and said: "My angel wife!
Whatever torment or disquietude
I may have suffered, you have never been

Its cause, or its occasion.　You are all—
You have been all, that womanhood can be
To manhood's want; and in your woman's love
And woman's pain, I have found every good
My life has known since first our lives were joined.
You knew me better than I knew myself;
And your prophetic words have haunted me
Like thoughts of retribution: ' *There will come*
' *A sad, sad time, when in your famished soul*
' *The cry for something more, and more divine*
' *Will rise, nor be repressed.*'　For something more
My spirit clamors: nothing more divine
I ask for."

　　　　　"What shall be this 'something more'?"

"Work," I replied; "ay, work, but never here;
Work among men, where I may feel the touch
Of kindred life; work where the multitudes
Are surging; work where brains and hands
Are struggling for the prizes of the world;
Work where my spirit, driven to its bent

By competitions and grand rivalries,
Shall vindicate its own pre-eminence,
And wring from a reluctant world the meed
Of approbation and respect for which
It yearns with awful hunger; work, indeed,
Which shall compel the homage of the souls
That creep around me here, and pity you
Because, forsooth, the Fates have hobbled you
With a dull drone.   I know how sweet the love
Of two fond souls ; and I will have the hearts
Of millions.   These shall satisfy my greed,
And round the measure of my life ; and these
My work shall win me."

At these childish words,
She raised her head, and with a sweet, sad smile
Of love and pity blent, made her response :
"Not yet, my husband—if your wife may speak
A thought that crosses yours—not yet have you
Found the great secret of content.   But work
May help you toward it, and in any case
Is better far than idleness.   For this,

You ask of me to sacrifice this home
And all the truest friends my life has gained.
I do it from this moment; glad to prove,
At any tender cost, my love for you,
And faith in your endeavor.   I will go
To any spot of earth where you may lead,
And go rejoicing.   Let us go at once!"

•

"I burn my ships behind me," I replied.
"Measure the cost: be sure no secret hope
Of late return be found among the flames;
For, if I go, I leave no single thread,
Save that which binds me to my mother's grave,
To draw me back."

       "My love shall be the torch
To light the fire," she answered.

          Then we rose,
And, with a kiss, marked a full period
To love's excess, and with a sweet embrace
Wrote the initial of a stronger life.

A REFLECTION.

Oh! not by bread alone is manhood nourished
    To its supreme estate!
By every word of God have lived and flourished
    The good men and the great.
      Ay, not by bread alone!

"Oh! not by bread alone!" the sweet rose, breathing
    In throbs of perfume, speaks;
" But myriad hands, in earth and air, are wreathing
    The blushes for my cheeks.
      Ay, not by bread alone!"

"Oh ! not by bread alone !" proclaims in thunder
      The old oak from his crest ;
" But suns and storms upon me, and deep under,
      The rocks in which I rest.
          Ay, not by bread alone !"

"Oh ! not by bread alone !"   The truth flies singing
      In voices of the birds ;
And from a thousand pastured hills is ringing
      The answer of the herds :
          " Ay, not by bread alone !"

Oh ! not by bread alone ! for life and being
      Are finely complex all,
And increment, with element agreeing,
      Must feed them, or they fall.
          Ay, not by bread alone !

Oh ! not by love alone, though strongest, purest,
      That ever swayed the heart ;
For strongest passion evermore the surest
      Defrauds each manly part.
          Ay, not by love alone !

Oh ! not by love alone is power engendered.
    Until within the soul
The gift of every motive has been rendered,
    It is not strong and whole.
      Ay, not by love alone !

Oh ! not by love alone is manhood nourished
    To its supreme estate :
By every word of God have lived and flourished
    The good men and the great.
      Ay, not by love alone!

8

KATHRINA.

PART III.

LABOR.

PART III.

_____

LABOR.

TEN years of love!—a sleep, a pleasant dream
That passed its culmen in the early half,
Concluding in confusion—a wild scene
Of bargains, auctions, partings, and what not?—
And an awaking!

                I was in Broadway,
A unit in a million.   Like a bath
In ocean surf, blown in from farthest seas
Under the August ardors, the grand rush
Of crested life assailed me with its waves,
And cooled me while it fired.   With sturdy joy

I sought its broadest billows, and resigned
My spirit to their surge and sway; or stood
In sheltered coves, reached only by the spume
And crepitant bubbles of the yesty floods,
Drinking the roar, the sheen, the restlessness,
As inspiration, both of sense and soul.

I saw the waves of life roll up the steps
Of great cathedrals and retire; and break
In charioted grandeur at the feet
Of marble palaces, and toss their spray
Of feathered beauty through the open doors,
To pile the restless foam within; and burst
On crowded caravansaries, to fall
In quick return; and in dark currents glide
Through sinuous alleys and the grimy loops
Of reeking cellars; and with softest plash
Assail the gilded shrines of opulence,
And slide in musical relapse away.

With senses dazed and stunned, and soul o'erfilled
With chaos of new thoughts, I turned away,

And sought my city home.   There all was calm,
With wife and daughter waiting my return,
And eager with their welcome.   That was life!—
An interest in the great world of life,
A place for toil within a world of toil,
And love for its reward.   "Amen!" I said,
"And twice amen! I've found my life at last,
And we will all be happy."

                              Day by day—
The while I sought adjustment to the life
Which I had chosen, and with careful thought
Gathered to hand the fair material
Elect by Fancy for the organism
Over whose germ she brooded—I went out,
To bathe again upon the shore of life
My long-enfeebled nature.

                              Every day
I met some face I knew.   My college friends
Came up in strange disguises.   Here was one,
With a white neck-cloth and a saintly face,

Who had been rusticated and disgraced
For lawlessness. Now he administered
A charge which proved that he had been at work,
And made himself a man. And there was one—
A lumpy sort of boy, as memory
Recalled him to me—grown to portliness
And splendid spectacles. He drove a chaise,
And practiced surgery,—was on his way
To meet a class of youth, who sought to be
Great surgeons like himself, and took full notes
Of all his stolen wisdom. By his watch—
A gold repeater, with a mighty chain—
He gave me just five minutes; then rolled off—
Pretension upon wheels. Another grasped
My hand as if I were his bosom friend,
Just in from a long voyage. He was one
Who stole my wood in college, and received
With grace the kick I gave him. He had grown
To be the tail of a portentous firm
Of city lawyers: managed, as he said,
The matter of collections; and had made
In his small way—to use his modest phrase:

Truthful as modest—quite a pretty plum.
He was o'erjoyed to see me in the town:
Hoped I would call upon him at his den:
If I had any business in his line,
Would do it for me promptly; as for price,
No need to talk of that between two friends!

But these, and all—the meanest and the best —
Were hard at work.   They always questioned me
Before we parted, touching my pursuits ;
And though they questioned kindly, I grew sore
Under the repetition, and ashamed
To iterate my answer, till I burned
To do some work, so lifted into fame,
That shame should be to him whose ignorance
Compelled a question.

                    Simplest foresters
Have learned the trick of woodland broods, that fly
In radiant divergence from the flash
Of death and danger, and, when all is still,

8*

Steal back to where their fellows bit the dust
For rendezvous.   And thus society
Follows the brutal instinct.   When the friends,
Who from her father's ruin fled amain,
Found out my wife, and learned that it was safe
To gather back to the old feeding-ground,
They came.   Her old home had become my own
And they were all delighted.   It was sweet
To have her back again ; and it was sad
To know that those who once were happy there,
Dispensing happiness, could come no more.

It had its modicum of earnestness, —
This talk of their's — and she received it all
With hearty courtesy, and yielded it
The unction of her charity, so far
That it was smooth and redolent to her.
The difference — the world-wide difference —
Between my wife and them was obvious ;
But she was generous through nature's gift
I fancied — could not well be otherwise ;
Although their fawning filled me with disgust.

Oh! fool and blind! not to perceive the Christ
That shone and spoke in her!

                  The hour approached—
The pre-determined time—when I should close
My study-door, and wrap my kindling brain
In the poetic dream which, day by day,
Was gathering consistence in my brain.
The quick, creative instinct in me plumed
Its pinions for the flight, and I could feel
The influx of fresh power ; but whence it came,
I did not question ; though it fired my heart
With the assurance of success.

                        I told
My dear companion of my hopeful plans
For winning fame, and making for myself
A lofty place ; but I could not inspire
Her heart with my ambition, or win o'er
Her judgment to my motive. She adhered
To her old theory, and gave no room

To any motive it did not embrace.
We argued much, but always argued wide,
And ended where we started.   Postulates
On which we stood in perfect harmony,
Were points of separation, out from which
We struck divergently, till sympathy,
That only lives by rhythm of thoughts and hearts,
Lay dead between us.

        "Man loves praise," I said.
"It is an appetence which He who made
The human soul, made to be satisfied.
It is a tree He planted.   If it grow
On that which feeds it, and become at last
Thrifty and fruitful, it is still His own,
With usury.   And if, in His intent,
This passion have no place among the powers
Of active life, why is it mighty there
From youngest childhood?   Pray you what is fame
But concrete praise?—the universal voice
Which bears, from every quarter of the earth,
Its homage to a name, that grows thereby

To be its own immortal monument,
Outlasting all the marble and the bronze
Which cunning fingers, since the world began,
Have shaped or stamped with story?   What is fame
But aggregate of praise?   And if it be
Legitimate to win, for sake of praise,
The praise of one, why not of multitudes?"

"Ay," she replied; "'tis true that men love praise;
And it is true that He who made the soul
Planted therein the love of praise, to be
A motive in its life—all true so far;
And so far we agree.   But motives all
Have their appropriate sphere and sway, like men
Who bear them in their breasts.   The love of praise
Fills life with fine amenities.   Not all
Who live have pleasant tempers, and not all
The gift of gracious manners, or the love
Of nobler motive, higher meed than praise.
The world is full of bears, who smooth their hair,
And glove their paws, and put on manly airs,
And hold our honey sacred, and our lives

Our own, because they hunger for our praise.
'Tis a fine thing for bears—this love of praise—
And those who deal with them ; and a good thing
For children, and for parents, teachers—all
Who have them in their keeping.   It may hold
A little mind to rectitude, until
It grow, and grow ashamed to yield itself
To such a petty motive.   Children all
Like sugar, and it may admit of doubt
Whether our praise or sugar sweetens more
Their petulant sub-acids ; but a man
Would choke in swallowing the compliment
Which we should pay him, were we but to say
'Go to !   Do some great deed, and you shall have
Your pay in sugar :—maple, mind you, now,
So you shall do it featly.'"

                            "Very good !"
I answered, "very good, indeed ! if we
Engage in talk for sport ; but argument
On themes like these must have the element
Of candor.   Highest truth, in certain lights,

May be ridiculous, and yet be truth.

Women are angels: just a little weak

And just a little wicked, it may be,

Yet still the sweetest beings in the world ;

But when one stands with apprehensive gasp

At verge of sternutation, or leaps off,

Projecting all her being in a sneeze,

Or snores with lips wide-parted, or essays

The 'double-quick,' we turn our eyes away

In sadness, that a creature so divine

Can be so shockingly ridiculous ;

Yet who shall say she's not an angel still?

Now you present to me the meanest face

Of a most noble truth.   I laugh with you

Over its sorry semblance ; but the truth

Is still divine, and claims our reverence.

The great King Solomon—and you believe

In Solomon—has said that a good name

Is more to be desired than much fine gold.

If a good name be matter of desire

Beyond all wealth—and you will pardon me

For holding to the record—it may stand

As a grand motive in the life of man,
To grand endeavor.   I have yet to learn
That Solomon addressed his words to bears,
Or little children.   I am forced to think
That you and I, and all who read his words,
Are those for whom he wrote."

                                    Rejoining she :
"A good may be the subject of desire,
And not be motive to achievement.   Life,
If I may speak the riddle, is a scheme
Of indirections.   My own happiness
Is something to desire ; and yet, I know
That I must win it by forgetting it
In ministry to others.   If I make
My happiness the motive of my work,
I spoil it by the taint of selfishness.
But are you sure that you do not presume
Somewhat too much, in claiming the desire
For a good name as motive of your life?
Greatness, not goodness, is the end you seek,
If I mistake you not ; and these are held,

In the world's thought, as two, and most distinct.
King Solomon was wise, but wiser He
Who said to those that loved and followed him,
'Who would be great among you, let him serve.'
The greatest men—and artists should be such,
For they are God's nobility and man's—
Should work from greatest motives.   Selfishness
Is never great, and moves to no great deeds.
To honor God, to benefit mankind,
To serve with lofty gifts the lowly needs
Of the poor race for which the God-man died,
And do it all for love—oh ! this is great !
And he who does this will achieve a name
Not only great but good."

                     " Not in this world,"
I answered her.   " I know too much of it.
The world is selfish ; and it never gives
Due credit to a motive which assumes
To be above its own.   If a man write,
It takes for granted that he writes for fame,

And judges him accordingly.   It holds
Of no account all other aims and ends ;
And visits with contempt the man who bears
A mission to his kind.   The critic pens
That twiddle with his work, or play with it
As cats with mice, are not remarkable
For gentle instincts ; and my name must live
By pens like these.   I choose to take the world
Just as I find it, and I pitch my tune
To the world's key, that it may sing my tune,
And sing for me.   Ay, and I take myself
Just as I find myself.   I do not love
The human race enough to work for it.
Having no motive of philanthropy,
I'll make pretense to none.   The love of praise
I count legitimate and laudable.
'Tis not the noblest motive in the world,
But it is good ; and it has won more fames
Than any other.   Surely, my good wife,
You would not shut me from it, and deprive
My power of its sole impulse."

"No; oh! no,"
She answered quickly.   "I am only sad
That it should be the captain of your host.
All creatures of the brain are the result
Of many motives and of many powers.
All life is such, indeed.   The power that leads—
The motive dominant—this stamps the work
With its own likeness.   Throughout all the world
Are careful souls, with careful consciences,
That pierce themselves with questionings and fears.
Because that, with the motives which are good,
And which alone they seek, a hundred come
They do not seek, and aye sophisticate
Their finest action.   They are wrong in this:
All motives bowing to one leadership,
And aiding its emprise, are one with it —
The same in trend, the same in terminus.
All the low motives that obey the law,
And aid the work, of one above them all,
Do holy service, and fulfill the end
For which they were designed.   The love of praise
Is not the lowest motive which can move

The human soul.   Nay, it may do good work
As a subordinate, and leave no soil
On whitest fabric, at whose selvage shines
The Master's broidered signature.   Although
You write for fame, think not you will escape
The press of other motives.   You love me ;
You love your child ; you love your pleasant home ;
You love the memory of one long dead.
These, joined with all those qualities of heart
Which make you dear to me, will throng around
The leader you appoint, and come and go
Under his banner ; and the work of God
Will thrive through these, the while your own goes on.
God will not be defrauded, nor yet man ;
And you, who like the Pharisees make prayer
At corners of the streets, for praise of men,
Will have reward you seek."

                         "Ay, verily!"
Responded I with laughter.   "Verily!
Though not a saint, I'll do a saintly work
For my own profit, and in spite of all

The selfishness that moves me.   Better, this,
Than I suspected.   My sweet casuist—
My gentle, learned, lovely casuist—
I thank you ; and I'll pay you more than thanks.
I'll promise that when these fine motives come,
And volunteer their service, they shall find
Welcome and entertainment, and a place
Within the rank and file, with privilege
Of quick promotion, so they show themselves
Motives of mettle."

                          This the type of talk
That passed between us.   I was not a fool
To count her wisdom worthless ; nor a God,
To work regeneration in myself.
That something which I longed for, to fill up
The measure of my good, was human praise ;
Yet I could see that she was wholly right,
And that she held within herself resource
Of satisfaction better than my own.
But I was quite content—content to know
I trod the average altitude of those

Within the paths of art, and had no aims
To be misconstrued or misunderstood
By Pride and Selfishness—that these, in truth,
Expected of me what I had to give.

Strange, how a man may carry in his heart,
From year to year—through all his life, indeed—
A truth, or a conviction, which shall be
No more a part of it, and no more worth
Than to his flask the cork that slips within!
Of this he learns by sourness of his wine,
Or muddle of its color; by the bits
That vex his lips while drinking; but he feels
No impulse in his hand to draw it forth,
And bid it crown and keep the draught it spoils.

I write this, here, not for its relevance
To this one passage of my story, but
Because there slipped into my consciousness
Just at this juncture, and would not depart,

A truth I carried there for many years,
Each minute seeing, feeling, tasting it,
Yet never touching it with an attempt
To draw it forth, and put it to its place.

One evening, when our usual theme was up,
I asked my wife in playful earnestness
How she became so wise. "You talk," I said,
"Like one who has survived a thousand years,
And drunk the wisdom of a thousand lives."

"Who lacketh wisdom, let him ask of God,
Who giveth freely and upbraideth not,"
Was her reply.

             "I never ask of God,"
I said. "So, while you take at second hand
His breathings to the artist, I will take
At second hand the wisdom that he gives
To you, his teacher."

             "Do you never pray?"

"Never," I answered her.   "I cannot pray:
You know the reason.   Never since the day
God shut his heart against my mother's prayer
Have I raised one petition, or been moved
To reverence."

                    Her long, dark lashes fell,
And from her eyes there dropped two precious tears
That bathed her folded hands.   She pitied me,
With tenderness beyond the reach of words.
I did not seek her pity.   I was proud,
And asked her if she blamed me.

                        "No," she said ;
"I have no right to blame you, and no wish.
I marvel only that a man like you
Can hold so long the errors of a boy.
I've looked—with how much longing, words of mine
Can never tell—for reason to restore
That priceless thing which passion stole from you,
And looked in vain."

                    Though piqued by the reproach

Her words conveyed, (unwittingly I knew),
I wished to learn where, in her theory
Of human life, my case had found a place ;
So, bidding pride aback, I questioned her.
" You are so wise in other things," I said,
"And read so well God's dealings with his own,
Perhaps you can explain this mystery
That clouds my life."

           "I know that God is good,"
She answered, " and, although my reason fail
To explicate the mystery that wraps
His providence, it does not shake my faith.
But this sad case of yours has seemed so plain,
That Reason well may spare the staff of Faith
To climb to its conclusions.   You are loved,
My husband : can you tell your wife for what ?"

"Oh ! modesty ! my dear ; hem ! modesty !
Spare me these blushes ! I have not at hand
The printed catalogue of qualities
Which give you inspiration, and decline
The personal rehearsal."

9

                                    "You mistake,"
She answered, smiling. "Not for modesty ;
And as for blushes, they're not patent yet.
But frankly, soberly, I ask you this :
Have you a quality of heart or brain
Which makes you lovable, and in my eyes
A man to be admired, that was not born
Quick in your blood? Pray, have you anything
Which you did not inherit? Who to me
Furnished my husband? By what happy law
Was all that was the finest, noblest, best
In those who gave you life, bestowed on you?
You have your father's form, your father's brain :
You have your mother's eyes, your mother's heart,
Those twain produced a man for me to love,
Out of themselves. I am obliged to them
For the most precious good the round earth holds,
Transmitted by a law that slew them both.
It was not sin, or shame, for them to die
Just as they died. They passed with whiter hands
Up to The Throne than he who wantonly
Murders a sparrow. When your mother prayed,

She prayed for the suspension of the law
By which from Eve, the mother of the race,
She had received the grace and loveliness
Which made her precious to your heart—the law
By which alone she could convey these gifts
To others of her blood.   Your daughter's face
Is beautiful, her soul is pure and sweet,
By largess of this law.   Could God subvert,
To meet her wish, though shaped in agony,
The law which, since the life of man began
In life of God, has kept the channel clear
For His own blood, that it might bless the last
Of all the generations as the first?
What could He more than give her liberty—
When reason lay in torture or in wreck,
And life was death—to part with stainless hand
The tie that held her from his loving breast?"

If God himself had dropped her words from heaven,
They had not reached with surer plummet-plunge
The depths of my conviction.   I was dumb;
I opened not my mouth ; but left her side,

And sought the crowded street.   I felt that all
Delusions, subterfuges, self-deceits,
By which my soul had shut itself from God,
Were stripped away, and that no barrier
Was interposed between us which was not
My own hand's building.   Never, nevermore,
Could I hold God in blame, or deem myself
A guiltless, injured creature.   I could see
That I was hard, implacable, unjust ;
And that by force of willful choice I held
Myself from God ; for no impulsion came
To seek his face and favor.   Nay, I feared
And fought such incidence, as enemy
Of all my plans.

                              So it became thenceforth
A problem with me how to separate
My new conviction from my life—to hold
A revolutionizing truth within,
And hold it yet so loosely, it should be
Like a dumb alien in a mural town—
No guest, but an intruder, who might bide,

By law or grace, but win no domicile,
And hold no power.

When I returned, that night,
My course was chosen, with such sense of guilt
I blushed before the calm, inquiring eyes
That met me at my threshhold ; but the theme
Was dropped just there. My gentle mentor read
The secret of the struggle and the sin,
And left me to myself.

At the set time,
I entered on my task. The discipline
Of early years told feebly on my work,
For dissipation and disuse of power
Had brought me back to infancy again.
My will was weak, my patience was at fault,
And in my fretful helplessness, I stormed
And sighed by turns ; yet still held in force
Determination, as reserve of will ;
And when I flinched or faltered, always fell
Back upon that, and saved my powers from rout.

Casting, recasting, till I found the germ
Of my conception putting forth its whorls
In orderly succession round the stem
Of my design, that straight and strong shot up
Toward inflorescence, my long work went on,
Till I was filled with satisfying joy.
This lasted for a little time, and then
There came reaction.   I grew tired of it.
My verses were as meaningless and stale
As doggrel of the stalls.   I marvelled much
That they could ever have beguiled my pride
Into self-gratulation, or done aught
But overwhelm me with contempt for them,
And the dull pen that wrote them.

                         I had hoped
To form and finish my projected work
Within, and by, myself,—to tease no ear
With fragmentary snatches of my song,
And call for no support from friendly praise
To reinforce my courage; but the stress
Of my disgust and my despair—the need,

Imperative and absolute, to brace myself
By some opinion borrowed for the nonce,
And bathe my spirit in the sympathy
Of some strong nature—mastered my intent,
And sent me for resource to her whose heart
Was ever open to my call.

                        She sat
Through the long hour in which I read to her,
Absorbed, entranced, as one who sits alone
Within a dim cathedral, and resigns
His spirit to the organ-theme, that mounts,
Or sinks in tremulous pauses, or sweeps out
On mighty pinions and with trumpet voice
Through labyrinthine harmonies, at last
Emerging, and through silver clouds of sound
Receding and receding, till it melts
In the blue depths of the empyrean.
It was not needful she should say a word ;
For in her glowing eyes and kindling face,
I caught the full assurance that my heart
Had yearned for ; but she spoke her hearty praise ;

And when I asked her for her criticism,
Bestowed it with such modest deference
To my opinion, as to spare my pride ;
Yet, with such subtle sense of harmony,
And insight of proportion, that I saw
That I should find no critic in the world
More competent or more severe.   I said,
Gulping my pride :   " Better this ordeal
In friendly hands, before the time of types,
Than afterward, in hands of enemies."

So, from that reading, it was understood
Between us that, whenever I essayed
Revising and retouching, I should know
Her intimate impressions, and receive
Her frank suggestions.   In this oversight
And constant interest of one whose mind
Was excellent and pure, and raised above
All motive to beguile me, I secured
New inspiration.

                            Weeks and months passed by

With gradient hopefulness, and strength renewed
At each renewal of the confidence
I had reposed in her; till I perceived
That I was living on her praise—that she
Held God's place in me and the multitude's.
And now, as I look back upon those days
Of difficult endeavor, I confess
That had she not been with me, I had failed—
Ay, foundered in mid-sea—my hope, my life,
The spoil of deep oblivion.

       At last
The work was done—the labored volume closed.
"I cannot make it better," I exclaimed.
"I can write better, but, before I write,
I must have recognition in the voice
Of public praise. A good paymaster pays
When work is finished. Let him pay for this,
And I will work again; but, till he pay,
My leisure is my own, and I will wait."

"And if he grudge your wage?" suggested she
To whom I spoke.

   9*

                              " I shall be finished too."

Came then the proofs and latest polishing
Of words and phrases — work I shared with her
To whom I owed so much ; and then the fear,
The deathly heart-fall, and the haunting dread
That go before exposure to the world
Of inmost life, and utmost reach of power
Toward revelation ;—then the shrinking spell,
When morbid love of self awaits in pain
The verdict it has courted.

                              But at last
The book was out.   My daughter's hand in mine—
Her careless feet, that thrilled with springing life,
Skipping the pavement — I walked down Broadway,
To ease the restlessness and cool the heat
That vexed my idle waiting.   As we passed
A showy window, filled with costly books,
My little girl exclaimed : " Oh father !   See !
There is your name !"

                              Straight all the bravery

Within my veins, at one wild heart-thump, dropped,
And I was limp as water ; but I paused,
And read the placard.   It announced my book
In characters of flame, with adjectives
My daring publisher had filched, I think,
From an old circus-broadside.

                             "Well!" thought I—
Biting my lip—"I'm in the market now !
How much—O ! rattling, roaring multitude !
O ! selfish, cheating, lying multitude !
O ! hawking, trading, delving multitude !—
How much for one man's hope, for one man's life?
What for his toil and pain ?—his heart's red blood?
What for his brains and breeding?   Oh how much
For one who craves your praises with your pence,
And dies with your denial?"

                            I went in,
And bought my book—not doubting I was first
To give response to my apostrophe.
The smug old clerk, who found his length of ear

Convenient as a pencil-rack, and thus
Made nature's wrath proclaim the praise of trade,
Wrapped my dear bantling well ; and, as he dropped
My dollar in his till, smiled languidly
Upon my little girl, and said to me—
To cheer me in my purchase—that the book
Was thought to be a deuced clever thing.
He never read such books : he had no time.
Indeed, he had no interest in them.
Still, other people had, and it was well,
For it helped trade along.

         It was for him—
A vulgar fraction of the integral
We speak of as "the people," and "the world"—
I had been writing !   Had he read my book,
And given it his praise, I should have been
Delighted, though I knew that his applause
Was worthless as his brooch.   I was a fool
Undoubtedly ; yet I could understand,
Better than e'er before, how separate
The artist is from such a soul as his—

What need of teachers and interpreters
To crumble in his pewter porringer
The rounded loaf, whose crust was adamant
To his weak fingers.

     The next morning's press
Was purchased early, though I read in vain
To find my reputation.   But at night,
My door-bell rang ; and I received a note
From one who edited an evening print,
(I had dined with him at my publisher's),
Inclosing a review, and venturing
The hope that I should like it.

     Cunning man !
He knew the tricks of trade, and was adroit.
My poem was "a revelation."   I had " burst
Like thunder from a calm and cloudless sky."
Well, not to quote his language, this the drift :
A man of fortune, living at his ease,
But fond of manly effort, had sat down,
And turned his culture to supreme account ;

And he — the editor — took on himself
To thank him on the world's behalf.   Withal,
The poet had betrayed the continence
Of genius.   He had held, undoubtedly,
The consciousness of power from early youth ;
But, yielding never to the itch for print,
Had nursed and chastened and developed it,
Until his hand was strong, and swept his lyre
With magic of a master.

                                        Followed here
Sage comments on the rathe and puny brood
Of poet-sucklings, who had rushed to type
Before their time — pale stems that spun their flowers
In the first sunshine, but, when Autumn came,
Were fruitless.   It was pleasant, too, to see,
In such an age of sentimental cant,
One man who dared to hold up to the world
A creature of his brain, and say : "Look you !
This is my thought ; and it shall stand alone.
It has no moral, bears no ministry
Of pious teaching, and makes no appeal

To sufferance or suffrage of the muffs
Who, in the pulpit or the press, prepare
The nation's pap. The fiery-footed barb
That pounds the pampas, and the lily-bells
That hang above the brooks, present the world
With no apology for being there,
And no attempt to justify themselves
In uselessness. It is enough for God
That they are beautiful, and hold his thought
In fine embodiment ; and it shall be
Enough for me that, in this book of mine,
I have created sowewhat that is strong
And beautiful, which, if it profit,—well :
If not, 'tis no less strong and beautiful,
And holds its being by no feebler right."

Ay, it was glorious to find one man
Who piled no packs upon his Pegasus,
Nor chained him to a rag-cart, loaded down
With moral frippery, and strings of bells
To call the people to their windows.

Then

There followed extracts, with a change of type
To mark the places where the editor
Had caught a fancy hiding, which he feared
Might slip detection under slower eyes
Than those he carried ; or to emphasize
Felicities of diction that were stiff
In Roman verticals, but grew divine
At the Italic angle ; then apology,
Profoundly humble, to his patrons all
For quoting at such length, and one to me
For quoting anything, and deep regrets,
In quite a general way, that lack of space
Forbade the reproduction of the book
From title-page to tail-piece, winding up
With counsel to all lovers of pure art,
Patrons of genius, all Americans,
All friends of cis-Atlantic literature,
To buy the book, and read it for themselves.

I drank the whole, at one long, luscious draught,
Tipping the tankard high, that I might see

My features at the bottom, and regale
My pride, after my palate.   Then I tossed
The paper to my wife, and bade her read.
I watched her while she read, but failed to find
The sympathy of pleasure in her face
I had expected.   Finishing at last,
She raised her eyes, and, fixing them on me,
Said thoughtfully: "You like this, I suspect."

"Well, rather!" I responded, "since it seems
To be the first installment of the wage
Which you suggested might come grudgingly.
Ay, it is sweet to me.   I know it fails
In nice discrimination,—that it slurs
Defects which I perceive as well as you;
But it is kind, and places in best light
Such excellences as we both may find—
May claim, indeed."

                              "And yet, it is a lie,
Or what the editor would call 'a puff,'
From first to last.   The 'continence,' my dear,
'Of genius!'   What of that?   And what about

The 'manly effort,' for whose exercise
He thanked you on the world's behalf?   And so
Your nursing, chastening and developing
Of power!—Pray what of these?"

      "Oh! wife!" I said;
"Don't spoil it all!   Be pitiful, my love!
I am a baby—granted: so I need
The touch of tender hands, and something sweet
To keep me happy."

      "Babies take a bath,
Sometimes, from which the hand of warmest love
Filches the chill, and you must have one dash,"
She answered me, "to close your complement.
The weakest spot in all your book, he found
With a quick instinct; and on that he spent
His sharpest force and finest rhetoric,
Shoring and bracing it on every side
With bold assumptions and affirmatives,
To blind the eyes of novices, and scare
With fierce forestallment all the critic-quills
Now bristling for their chance.   He saw at once

Your poem had no mission, save, perhaps,
The tickle of the taste, and that it bore
Upon its glowing gold small food for life.
He saw just there the point to be attacked ;
And there threw up his earth-works, and spread out
His thorned abattis.   He was very kind
Undoubtedly, and very cunning, too ;
For well he knew that there are earnest souls
In the broad world, who claim that highest art
Is highest ministry to human need ;
And that the artist has no Chistian right
To prostitute his art to selfish ends,
Or make it vehicle alone of plums
For the world's pudding."

                    "These will speak in time,"
Responded I ; " but they have not the ear
Of the broad world, I think.   The Christian right
Of which you speak is hardly recognized
Among the multitude, or by the guild
In which I claim a place.   The sectaries
Who furnish folios, quartos, magazines,

To the religious few, are limited
In influence ; and these, my wife, are all
I have to fear ;—nay, could I but arouse
Their bitter enmity, I might receive
Such superflux of praise and patronage
As would o'erwhelm my sweetly Christian wife
With shame and misery.   But we shall see ;
And, in the meantime, let us be content
That, if one man shall praise me overmuch,
Ten, at the least, will fail to render me
Befitting justice."

                    As the days went on,
Reviews and notices came pouring in.
I was notorious, at least ; and fame,
I whispered comfortably to myself,
Is only notoriety turned gray,
With less of fire, if more of steadiness.
The adverse verdicts were not numerous ;
And these were rendered, as I fancied then,
By sanctimonious fools who deemed profane
All verse outside their thumb-worn hymnodies.

My book received the rattling fusilade
Of all the dailies : then the artillery
Of the hebdomadals, whose noisy shells,
Though timed by fuse to burst on Saturday,
Exploded at the middle of the week ;
And last, a hundred-pounder quarterly
Gave it a single missive from its mask
Of far and dark impersonality.
The smoke cleared up, and still my colors flew,
And still my book stood proudly in the sun,
Nor breached nor battered.

                    I had won a place :
That I was sure of.   All had said of me
That I was " brilliant :" was not that enough?
The petty pesterers, with card and stamp,
Who hunt for autographs, were after me,
In packages by post ; and idle men
Held me at corners by the button-hole,
And introduced me to their friends.   I dined
With meek-eyed men, whose literary wives
Were dying all to know me, as they said ;

And the lyceums, quick at scent and sight—
Watching the jungles for a lion—all
Courted the delectation of my roar
Upon their platforms, pledging to my hand
(With city reference to stanchest names),
Such honoraria as would have been
The lion's share of profits.   These were straws ;
But they had surer fingers for the wind
Than withes or weathercocks.

                              The book sold well,
My publisher (who published at my risk),
And first put on the airs of one who stooped
To grant a favor, brimmed and overflowed
With courtesy ; and ere a year was gone,
Became importunate for something more.
This was his plea : I owed it to myself
To write again.   The time to make one's hay
Is when the sun shines : time to write one's books
Is when the public humor turns to them.
The public would forget me in a year,
And seek another idol ; or, meanwhile,

Another writer might usurp my throne,
And I be hooted from my own domain
As a pretender.   Then the market's maw
Was greedy for my poems.   Just how long
The appetite would last, he could not tell,
For appetite is subject of caprice,
And never lasts too long.

                The man was wise,
I plainly saw, and gave me the results
Of observation and experience.
I took his hint, accepting with a pang
The truths that came with it: for instance, these:—
That he who speaks for praise of those who live,
Must keep himself before his audience,
Nor look for "bravas," cheers, and cries of "hear!"
And clap of hands and stamp of feet, except
With fresh occasion; that applause of crowds,
Though fierce, runs never to the chronic stage;
That good paymasters, having paid for work
The doer's price, expect receipt in full
At even date; and that if I would keep

My place, as grand purveyor to the greed
For novelties of literary art,
My viands must be sapid, and abound
With change, to wake or whet the appetite
I sought to feed.

                    I say I took his hint,
Bestowed in selfishness, without a doubt,
Though in my interest.   For ten long years
It was the basis of my policy.
I poured my poems with redundancy
Upon the world, and won redundant meed.
If I gave much, the world was generous,
Repaying more than justice : but, at last,
Tired and disgusted, I laid down my pen.
I knew my work would not outlast my life,
That the enchantments which had wreathed themselves
Around my name were withering away,
With every breath of fragrance they exhaled ;
And that, too soon, the active brain and hand
Whose skill had conjured them, would faint and fail
Under the press of weariness and years.

My reputation piqued me. None believed
That it was in me to write otherwise
Than I had written. All the world had laughed,
Or shaken its wise head, had I essayed
A work beyond the round of brilliancies
In which my pen had reveled, and for which
It gave such princely guerdon. If I looked,
Or came to look, with measureless contempt
On those who gave with such munificence
The boon I sought, I had provoking cause.
I fooled them all with patent worthlessness,
And they insisted I should fool them still.
The wisdom of a whole decade had failed
To teach them that the thing my hand had done
Was not worth doing.

            More and worse than this:
I found my character and self-respect
Eroded by the canker of conceit,
Poisoned by jealousy, and made the prey
Of meanest passions. Harlequins in mask,
Who live upon the laughter of the throng

10

That crowds their reeking amphitheaters ;
Light-footed dancing-girls, who sell their grace
To gaping lechers of the pit, to win
That which shall feed their shameless vanity ;
The mimics of the buskin—baser still,
The mimics of the negro—minstrel-bands,
With capital of corks and castanets
And threadbare jests—Ah ! who and what was I
But brother of all these—in higher walk,
But brother in the motive of my life,
In jealousy, in recompense for toil,
And, last, in destiny ?

                              My wife had caught
Stray silver in her hair in these long years ;
And the sweet maiden springing from our lives
Had grown to womanhood.   In my pursuits,
Which drank my time and my vitality,
I had neglected them.   I worked at home,
But lived in other scenes, for other lives,
Or, rather, for my own ; and though my pride

Shrank from the deed, I had the tardy grace
To call them to me, and confess my shame,
And beg for their forgiveness.

                              Once again—
An explanations passed—I sat beside
My faithful wife, and canvassed as of old
New plans of life.   I found her still the same
In purpose and in magnanimity;
For she dealt no upbraidings and no blame;
Cast in my teeth no old-time phophecies
Of failure; felt no triumph which rejoiced
To mock me with the words, "I told you so."
Calmly she sat, and tried, with gentlest speech,
To heal the bruises of my fall; to wake
A better feeling in me toward the world,
And soothe my morbid self-contempt.

                              The world,
She said, is apt to take a public man
At his own estimate, and yield him place

According to his choice.   I had essayed
To please the world, and gather in its praise ;
And, certainly, the world was pleased with me,
And had not stinted me in its return
Of plauditory payment.   As the world
Had taken me according to my rate,
And filled my wish, it had a valid claim
On my good nature.

               Then, beyond all this,
The world was not a fool.   Those books of mine,
That I had come to look upon as trash,
Were not all trash.   My motive had been poor,
And that had vitiated them for me ;
But there was much in them that yielded strength
To struggling souls, and, to the wounded, balm.
Indeed, she had been helped by them, herself.
They were all pure ; they made no foul appeal
To baseness and brutality ; they had
An element of gentle chivalry,
Such as must have a place in any man
Shrinking with sensitiveness, like myself,

From a fine reputation, scorning it
For motive which had won it.

Words like these,
From lips like hers, were needed medicine.
They clarified my weak and jaundiced sight,
And helped to juster vision of the world,
And of myself. But there was no return
Of the old greed ; and fame, which I had learned
To be an entity quite different
From my conceit of it in other days,
Was something much too far and nebulous
To be my star of life.

"You have some plan ?"—
Statement and query in same words, which fell
From lips that sought to rehabilitate
My will and self-respect.

"I have," I said.

"Else you were dead," responded she. "To live,

Men must have plans.   When these die out of men
They crumble into chaos, or relapse
Into inanity.   Will you reveal
These plans of yours to me?"

                              "Ay, if I can,"
I answered her; "but first I must reveal
The base on which I build them.   I have tried
To find the occasion of my discontent,
And find it, as I think, just here : In quest
Of popularity, I have become
Untrue both to myself and to my art.
I have not dared to speak the royal truth
For fear of censure : I have been a slave
To men's opinions.   What is best in me
Has been debauched by the pursuit of praise
As life's best prize.   Conviction, sentiment,
All love and hate, all sense of right and wrong,
I have held in abeyance, or compelled
To work in menial subservience
To my grand purpose.   If my sentiment
Or my conviction were but popular,

It flowed in hearty numbers : otherwise,
It slept in silence.

"Now as to my art :
I find that it has suffered like myself,
And suffered from same cause.   My verse has been
Shaped evermore to meet the people's thought.
That which was highest, grandest in my art
I have not reached, and have not tried to reach.
I have but touched the surfaces of things
That meet the common vision ; and my art
Has only aimed to clothe them gracefully
With fancy's gaudy fabrics, or portray
Their patent beauties and deformities.
Above the people in my gift and art,
Both gift and art have had a downward trend
And both are prostitute.

"Discarding praise
As motive of my labor, I confess
My sins against my art, and so, henceforth,
As to my goddess, give myself to her.

The chivalry which you are pleased to note
In me and works of mine, turns loyally
To her and to her service.   Nevermore
Shall pen of mine demean itself by work
That serves not first, and with supreme intent,
The art whose slave it is."

    " I understand,
I think, the basis of your plan," she said ;
"And e'en the plan itself.   You now propose
To write without remotest reference
To the world's wishes, prejudices, needs,
Or e'en the world's opinions,— quite content
If the world find aught in you to applaud ;
Quite as content if it condemn.   With full
Expression of yourself, in finest terms
And noblest forms of art, so far as God
Has made you masterful, you give yourself
Up to yourself and to your art.   Is this
Fair statement of your purpose?"

    " Not unfair,"
I answered.   "Tell me what you think of it.'

"Suppose," she said, "that all the artist-souls
That God has made since time and art began
Had acted on your theory: suppose
In architecture, picture, poetry,
Naught had found utterance but works that sprang
To satisfy the worker, and reveal
That bundle of ideas which, to him,
Is constituted art ; but which, in truth,
Is figment of his fancy, or his thought,—
His creature, made his God—say where were all
The temples, palaces and homes of men ;
The galleries that blaze with history,
Or bloom with landscape, or look down
With smile of changeless love or loveliness
Into the hearts of men?   And where were all
The poems that give measure to their praise,
Voice to their aspirations, forms of light
To homely facts and features of their life,
Enveloping this plain, prosaic world
In an ideal atmosphere, in which
Fair angels come and go?   All gifts of men
Were made for use, and made for highest use.

If highest use be service of one's self,
And highest standard, one's embodiment
Of dogmas, theories and thoughts of art,
As art's identity, then are you right ;
But if a higher use of gift and art
Be service of mankind, and higher rule
God's regal truth, revealed in words or worlds,
And verified by life, then are you wrong."

" But art?"—responded I—" you do not mean
That art is nothing but a thing of thought,
Or, less than that, of fancy? Nay, I claim
That it is somewhat—a grand entity—
An organism of lofty principles,
Informed with subtlest life, and clothed upon
With usage and tradition of the men
Who, working in those sunny provinces
Where it holds eminent domain, have brought
To build its temple and adorn its walls
The usufruct of countless lives.   So far
Is art from being creature of man's thought
That it is subject of his knowledge—stands

In mighty mystery, and challenges
The study of the world ; rules noblest minds
Like law or like religion ; is a power
To which the proudest artist-spirits bow
With humblest homage. Is astronomy
The creature of man's thought? Is chemistry?
Yet these hold not, in this our universe,
A form more definite, nor yet a place
In human knowledge more beyond dispute,
Than art itself. To this embodiment
Of theory — of dogmas, if you will —
This body aggregate of truth revealed
In growing light of ages to the eyes
Touched to perception, I devote my life."

" Nay, you're too fast," she said : " let alchemy
And old astrology present your thought.
These were somewhat ; these were grand entities ;
But they went out like candles in thin air
When knowledge came. The sciences are things
Of law, of force, relations, measurements,
Affinities and combinations, all

The definite, demonstrable effects
Of first and second causes.   Between these
And men's opinions, braced by usages,
The space is wide.   The thing which you call art,
Is anything but definite in form,
Or fixed in law.   It has as many shapes
As worshipers.   The world has many books,
Written by earnest men, about this art;
But having read them, we are no more wise
Than he whose observation of the sun
Is taken by kaleidoscope.   The more
He sees in it, the more he is confused.
The sun works, doubtless, many fine effects
With what he sees, but he sees not the sun."

" But art is art," I said.   " You'd cheat my sense,
And mock my reason too.   Ay, art is art.
Things must have being that have history."

Then she :   " Yes, politics has history,
And therefore has a being,—has, in truth,
Just such a being as I grant to art—

A being of opinions.   Every state
Has origin and ends of government
Peculiarly its own, and so, from these,
Constructs its theory of politics,
And holds this theory against the world :
And holds it well.   There is no fixedness
Or form of politics for all mankind ;
And there is none of art.   Each artist-soul
Is its own law; and he who dares to bring
From work of other man, to lay on yours,
His square and compasses—declaring him
The pattern man—and tells, by him, you lack
Just so much here, or wander so much there,
Thereby confesses just how much he lacks
Of wisdom and plain sense.   For every man
Has special gift of power and end of life.
No man is great who lives by other law
Than that which wrapped his genius at his birth.
The Lind is great because she is the Lind,
And not the Malabran.   Recorded art
Is yours to study—e'en to imitate,
In education—imitate or shun,

As the case warrants; but it has destroyed,
Or toned to commonplace, more gifts of God
Than it has ever fanned to life or fed.
Who never walks save where he sees men's tracks
Makes no discoveries.   Show me the man
Who, leaving God and nature and himself,
Sits at the feet of masters, stuffs his brain
With maxims, notions, usages and rules,
And yields his fancy up to leading-strings,
And I shall see a man who never did
A deed worth doing.   So, in the name of art —
Nay, in the name of God — do no such thing
As smutch your knees by bowing at a shrine,
Whose doubtful deity, in midst of dust,
Sits in the cast-off robes of devotees,
And lives on broken victuals!"

                    "Drive, my dear!
Drive on, and over me!   You're on the old
High-stepping horse to-night; so give him rein,
For exercise is good," I said, in mirth.
"You sit your courser finely.   I confess

I'm very proud of you, and too much pleased
With your accomplishments to check your speed.
Drive on, my love! drive on!"

"I thank you, sir!
No one so gracious as your grudging man
Under compulsion!   With your kind consent
I'll ride a little further," she replied,—
"For I enjoy it quite as much as you—
The more because you've given me little chance
In these last years. . . . . Now, soberly, this art—
Of which we talk so much, without the power
To tell exactly what we understand
By the hack term—suppose we take the word,
And try to find its meaning.   You recall
Old John who dressed the borders in our court:
You called him, hired him, told him what to do.
He and his rake stood interposed between
You and your work.   You chose his skillful hands,
Endowing them with pay, or pledge of pay,
And set him at his labor.   Now suppose
Old John had had a philosophic turn

After you left him, and had thought like this:
'I am called here to do a certain work—
My rake tells what; and he who called me here
Has given me the motive for the job.
The work is plain. These borders are to be
Leveled and cleaned of weeds : my hand and rake
Are fitted for the service ;—this my art ;
And it is first of all the arts. There's none
More ancient, useful, worshipful, indeed,
Than agriculture. Adam practiced it ;
Poets have sung its praises ; and the great
Of every age have loved and honored it.
This art is greater than the man I serve,
And greater than his borders. Therefore I
Will serve my art, and let the borders lie,
And my employer whistle. True to that,
And to myself, it matters not to me
. What weeds may grow, or what the master think
Of my proceeding!'

      "So, intent on this,
He hangs his rake upon your garden wall,

And steals your clematis, with which to wind
The handle upward ; then o'erfills his hands
With roses and geraniums, and weaves
Their beauty into laurel, for a crown
For his slim god, completing his *devoir*
By buttering the teeth, and kneeling down
In abject homage.   Pray, what would you say,
At close of day, when you should go to see
Your untouched borders, and your gardener
At genuflexion, with your mignonnette
In every button-hole?   Remember, now,
He has been true to art and to himself,
According to his notion ; nor forget
To take along a dollar for his hire,
Which he expects, of course !   What would you say ?"

"Oh don't mind that : you've reached your 'fifthly' now,
And here the 'application' comes," I said.

"I think," responded she, with an arch smile,
"The application's needless : but you men
Are so obtuse, when will is in the way,

That I will do your bidding.   Every gift

That God bestows on men holds in itself

The secret of its office, like the rake

The gardener wields.   The rake was made to till—

Was fashioned, head and handle, for just that;

And if, by grace of God, you hold a gift

So fashioned and adapted, that it stands

In like relation of supremest use

To life of men, the office of your gift

Has perfect definition.   Gift like this

Is yours, my husband.   In your facile hands

God placed it for the service of himself,

In service of your kind.   Taking this gift,

And using it for God and for the world,

In your own way, and in your own best way;

Seeking for light and knowledge everywhere

To guide your careful hand ; and opening wide

To spiritual influx all your soul,

That so your master may breathe into you,

And breathe his great life through you, in such forms

Of pure presentment as he gives you skill

To build withal—that's all of art—for you.

Art is an instrument, and not an end—
A servant, not a master, nor a God
To be bowed down to.   Shall we worship rakes?
Honor of art, by him whose work is art,
Is a fine passion; but he honors most
Whose use and end are best."

                              "Use! Use! Use!"
I cried impatiently;—"nothing but use!
As if God never made a violet,
Or hung a harebell, or in kindling gold
Garnished a sunset, or upreared the arch
Of a bright rainbow, or endowed a world—
A universe, indeed—stars, firmament,
The vastitudes of forest and of sea,
Swift brooks and sweeping rivers, virid meads
And fluff of breezy hills—with tints that range
The scale of spectral beauty, till they leave
No glint or glory of the changeful light
Without a revelation!   Is this use—
I beg your pardon, love: you say 'this art'—
The sum and end of art?   If it be so,

Then God's no artist. Are the crystal brooks
Sweeter for singing to the thirsty brutes
That dip their beaded muzzles in the foam?
Burns the tree better that its leaves are green?
Sleeps the sun sounder under canopy
Of gold or rose ?"

"Yet beauty has its use,"
Responded she. "Whatever elevates,
Inspires, refreshes, any human soul,
Is useful to that soul. Beauty has use
For you and me. The dainty violet
Blooms in our thought, and sheds its fragrance there ;
And we are gainers through its ministry.
All God's great values wear the drapery
That most becomes them. Beauty may, in truth,
Be incident of art and not be end—
Its form, condition, features, dress, and still
The humblest value of the things of art.
This truth obtains in all God's artistry.
Does God make beauty for himself, alone?
He is, and holds, all beauty. Has he need

To kindle rushes that he may behold
The glory of his thoughts? or need to use
His thoughts as plasms for the amorphous clay
That he may study models? For an end
Outside himself, he ever speaks himself;
And end, with him, is use."

         "Well, I confess
There's truth in what you utter," I replied;—
"A modicum of truth, at least; and still
There's something more which this our subtle talk
Has failed to give us. I will not affirm
That art, recorded in its thousand forms,
And clothed with usages, traditions, rules,—
The thing of history—the mighty pile
Of drift that sweep of ages has brought down
To heap the puzzled present—is the sum
And substance of all art. I will not claim—
Nay, mark me now—I will not even claim
That beauty is art's end, or has its end
Within itself. Our tedious colloquy
Has cleared away the rubbish from my thought,

And given me cleaner vision.   I can see
Before, around me, underneath, above,
The great unrealized; and while I bow
To the traditions and the things of art,
And hold my theories, I find myself
Inspired supremely by the Possible
That calls for revelation—by the forms
That sleep imprisoned in the snowy arms
Of still unquarried truth, or stretch their hands
At sound of sledge and drill and booming fire,
Imploring for release.   I turn from men,
And stretch my hands toward these.   I feel—I know—
That there are mighty myriads waiting there,
And listening for my steps.   Suppose my age
Should fail to give them welcome: ay, suppose
They may not help a man to coin a dime
Or cook a dinner: they will fare as well
As much of God's truth fares, though clothed in forms
Divinely chosen.   Does God ever stint
His utterance because no creature hears?
Is it a grand and goodly thing, to spend

Brave life and precious treasure in a search
For palpitating water at the pole,
That so the sum of knowledge may be swelled,
Though pearls are not increased ; and something less
To probe the Possible in art, or sit
Through months of dreary dark to catch a glimpse
Of the live truth that quivers with the jar
Of movement at its axle?   Is it good
To garner gain beyond the present need,
Won by excursive commerce in all seas ;
And something less to pile redundantly
The spoil of thought?"

"These latest words of yours,"
She answered musingly, "impress me much ;
And yet, I think I see where they will lead,
Or, rather, fail to lead.   Your fantasy
Is beautiful but vague.   The Possible
Is a vast ocean, from which one poor soul,
With its slight oars, can float but flimsy freight ;
Yet I would help your courage, for I see

Where your sole motive lies.   Go on, and prove
Whether your scheme or mine holds more of good ;
And take my blessing with you."

                   Then she rose,
And kissed my forehead.   Looking in her face,
By the sharp light that touched her, I was thrilled
By her flushed cheeks and strangely lustrous eyes.
She spoke not ; but I heard the sigh she breathed —
The long-drawn, weary sigh — as she retired ;
And then the Possible, which had inspired
So wondrously my hope, drooped low around,
And filled me with foreboding.

                  Had her life
Been chilled by my neglect?   Was it on wane?
Could she be lost to me?   Oh! then I felt,
As I had never felt before, how mean
Beside one true affection is the best
Of all earth's prizes, and how little worth
The world would be without her love — herself!

But sleep refreshed her, and next morn she sat

At our bright board, in her accustomed place;
And sunlight was not sweeter than her smile,
Or cheerfuller. My quick fears died away;
And though I saw that she had lost the fire
Of her young life, I comforted myself
With thinking that it was the same with me—
The sure result of years.

My time I gave
To my new passion, rioting at large
In the fresh realm of fancy and of thought
To which the passion bore me, and from which
I strove to gather for embodiment
Material of art.

The more I dreamed,
The broader grew my dream. The further on
My footsteps pushed, the brighter grew the light;
Till, half in terror, half in reverence,
I learned that I had broached the Infinite!
I had not thought my Possible could bear
Such name as this, or wear such attribute;

And shrank befitting distance from the front
Of awful secrets, hid in awful flame,
That scorched and scared me.

              So, more humble grown,
And less adventurous, I chose, at last,
My theme and vehicle of song, and wrote.
My faculties, grown strong and keen by use,
Bent to their task with earnest faithfulness,
And glowed with high endeavor. All of power
I had within me flowed into my hand ;
And learning, language — all my life's resource —
Lay close around my enterprise, and poured
Their hoarded wealth of imagery and words
Faster than I could use it. For long weeks,
My ardent labor crowded all my days,
Invaded sleep, and haunted e'en my dreams:
And then the work was done.

              I left it there,
And sought for recreative rest in scenes
That once had charmed me — in society
Where I was welcome: but the common talk

Of daily news—of politics and trade—
Was senseless as the chatter of the jays
In autumn forests.   No refreshing balm
Came to me in the sympathy of men.
In my retirement, I had left the world
To go its way; and it had gone its way,
And left me hopelessly.

                 I told my wife
Of my dissatisfaction and disgust,
But found small comfort in her words.   She said:
"The world is wide, and woman's vision short;
But I have never seen a man who turned
His efforts from his kind, and failed to spoil
All men for him—himself, indeed, for them;
And he who gives nor sympathy nor aid
To the poor race from which he seeks such boon,
Must be rejoiced if it be generous;
Content, if it be just.   Society
Is a grand scheme of service and return.
We give and take; and he who gives the most,
In ways directest, wins the best reward."

By purpose, I closed eyes upon my work
For many weeks, resisting every day
The impulse to review the glowing dream
My fancy had engendered: for I wished
To go with faculty and fancy cooled
To its perusal.   I had strong desire,
So far as in me lay, to see the work
With the world's eyes, for reasons—ah! I shrink
From writing them!   All men are sometimes weak,
And some are inconsistent with their wills.
If I were one of these, think not I failed
To justify my weakness to myself,
In ways that saved my pride.

                                Yet this was true:
I had an honest wish to learn how far
My work of heat had power to re-inspire
The soul that wrought it, and how well my verse
Had clothed and kept the creature of my thought;
For memory still retained the loveliness
That filled the fresh conceit.

When, in good time.
Rest and diversion had performed their work,
And the long fever of my brain was gone,
I broached my feast, first making fast my door.
That so no eye should mark my greedy joy
Or my grimaces, — doubtful of the fate
That waited expectation.

It were vain
To try, in these tame words, to paint the pang,
The faintness and the chill, which overwhelmed
My disappointed heart.   My welded thoughts
Which, in their whitest heat, had bent and bound
My language to themselves, imparting grace
To stiffest words, and meanings fresh and fine
To simplest phrases, interfusing all
With their own ardency, and shining through
With smoothly rounded beauty, lay in heaps
Of cold, unmeaning ugliness.   My words
Had shrunk to old proportions, and stood out

In hard, stiff angles, challenging a guess
Of what they covered.

               Meaningless to me,
Who knew the meaning that had once informed
Its faithless numbers, what way could I hope
That, to my own, or any future age,
My work should speak its full significance?
My latest child, begot in manly joy,
Conceived in purity, and born in toil,
Lay dead before me,—dead, and in the shroud
My hopeful hands had woven and bedecked
To be its chrisom.

             Then the first I learned
Where language finds its bound,—learned that beyond
The range of human commerce, save by force,
It never moves, nor lingers in the realm
It thus invades, a moment, if the voice
Of human commerce speak not the demand ;—
That language is a thing of use ;—that thought
Which seeks a revelation, first must seek

Adjustment in the scale of human need,
Or find no fitting vehicle.

And more :
That the great Possible which lies outside
The range of commerce is identical
With the stupendous Infinite of God,
Which only comes in glimpses, or in hints
Of vague significance, so dim, so vast,
That subtlest, most prehensile language, shrinks
From plucking of its robes, the while they sweep
The perfumed air '

I closed my manuscript,
And locked it in my desk.   Then stealing forth,
I sought the bustle of the street, to drown
In the great roar of careless toil, the pain
That brings despair.   My last resource was gone;
And as I brooded o'er the awful blank
Of hopeless life that waited for my steps,
A fear which I had feared to entertain
Found entrance to my heart, and held it still,
Almost to bursting.

                              Not alone my life
Was sliding from me; for my better life,
My pearl of price, the jewel in my crown,
My wife Kathrina, growing lovelier
With every passing day, arose each morn
From wasting dreams to paler loveliness,
And sank in growing weariness each night,
And hotter hectic, to her welcome bed.
Her bed!   The sweet, the precious nuptial bed!
Bed sanctified by love!   Bed blest of God
With fruit immortal!   Bed too soon to be
Crowned with the glory of a Christian death!
Ah God!   How it brought back the agony,
And the rebellious hate of other years —
The hopeless struggle of my will with Him
Whose will is law!

                         Thus torn with mingled thoughts
Of fear, despair and spite, I wore away
Miles of wild wandering about the streets,
Till weariness at last compelled my feet
To drag me to my home.

Before my door
Stood the familiar chair of one whose call
Was ominous of ill.   My heart grew sick
With flutter of foreboding and foredoom ;
But in swift silence I flew up the steps,
And, blind with stifled frenzy, reached the side
Of my poor wife.   She smiled at seeing me,
But I could only kneel, and bathe her hands
With tears and kisses.   In her gentle breast —
True home of love, and love and home to me —
The blood had burst its walls, and flowed in flame
From lips it left in ashes.

In her smile
Of perfect trustfulness, I caught first glimpse
Of that aureola of fadeless light
Which spans my lonely couch, and kindles hope
That when my time shall come to follow her,
My spirit may go out, enwreathed and wrapped
By the familiar glory, which to-night
Shall brood o'er all my vigils and my dreams!

11*

DESPAIR.

Ah! what is so dead as a perished delight!
 Or a passion outlived! or a scheme overthrown!
Save the bankrupt heart it has left in its flight,
 Still as quick as the eye, but as cold as a stone!

The honey-bee hoards for its winter-long need,
 The treasure it gathers in joy from the flowers;
And drinks in each sip of its silvery mead
 The flavor and flush of the sweet summer hours.

But a pleasure expires at its earliest breath:
 No labor can hoard it, no cunning can save;
For the song of its life is the sigh of its death,
 And the sense it has thrilled is its shroud and its grave.

Ah! what is our love, with its tincture of lust,
  And its pleasure that pains us and pain that endears,
But joy in an armful of beautiful dust
  That crumbles, and flies on the wings of the years?

And what is ambition for glory and power,
  But desire to be reckoned the uppermost fool
Of a million of fools, for a pitiful hour,
  And be cursed for a tyrant, or kicked for a tool?

Nay, what is the noblest that art can achieve,
  But to conjure a vision of light to the eyes,
That will pale ere we paint it, and pall ere we leave
  On the heart it betrays and the hand it defies?

We love, and we long with an infinite greed
  For a love that will fill our deep longing, in vain:
The cup that we drink of is pleasant, indeed,
  Yet it holds but a drop of the heavenly rain.

We plan for our powers the divinest we can;
  We do with our powers the supremest we may;

And, winning or losing, for labor and plan
　　The best that we garner is—rest and decay!

Content — satisfaction — who wins them?　Look down!
　　They are held without thought by the dolts and the
　　　　drones:
'Tis the slave who in carelessness carries the crown;
　　And the hovels have kinglier men than the thrones.

The maid sings of love to the hum of her wheel;
　　And her lover responds as he follows his team;
They wed, and their children come quickly to seal
　　In fulfillment the pledge of their loftiest dream.

With humblest ambitions and homeliest fare,
　　Contented, though toiling, they travel abreast,
Till the kind hand of death lifts their burden of care,
　　And they sink, in the faith of their fathers, to rest.

Did I beg to be born?　Did I seek to exist?
　　Did I bargain for promptings to loftier gains?
Did I ask for a brain, with contempt of the fist
　　That could win a reward for its labor and pains?

Was it kind—the strong promise that girded my youth?
　Was it good—the endowment of motive and skill?
Was it well to succeed, when success was, in truth,
　But the saddest of failure? Make answer, who will!

Do I rave without reason? Why, look you, I pray!
　I have won all I sought of the highest and best;
But it brings me no guerdon; and hopeless, to-day,
　I am poorer than when I set out on the quest.

Oh! emptiness! Life, what art thou but a lie,
　Which I greeted and honored with hopefulest trust?
Bah! the beautiful apples that tempted my eye
　Break dead on my tongue into ashes and dust!

"A Father who loves all the children of men"?
　"A future to fill all these bottomless gaps"?
But one life has failed: can I fasten again
　With my faith and my hope to a specious Perhaps?

O! man who begot me! O! woman who bore!
　Why, why did you call me to being and breath?
With ruin behind me, and darkness before,
　I have nothing to long for, or live for, but death!

KATHRINA.

PART IV.

CONSUMMATION.

PART IV.

CONSUMMATION.

A GUEST was in my house—a guest unbid—
Who stayed without a welcome from his host ;—
So loathed and hated, on such errand bent,
And armed with such resistless power of ill,
I dared not look him in the face.   I heard
His tireless footsteps in the lonely halls,
In the chill hours of night; and, in the day,
They climbed the stairs, or loitered through the rooms
With lawless freedom.   Ever when I turned
I caught a glimpse of him.   His shadow stalked
Between me and the light, and fled before
My restless feet, or followed close behind.

Whene'er I bent above the couch that held
My fading wife, though looking not, I knew
That he was bending from the other side,
And mocking me.

                Familiar grown, at last,
He came more closely—came and sat with me
Through hours of revery ; or, as I paced
My dimly-lighted room, slipped his lank arm
Through mine, and whispered in my shrinking ear
Such fearful words as made me sick and cold.
He took the vacant station at my board,
Sitting where she had sat, and mixed my cup
With poisoned waters, saying in low tones
That none but I could hear :

                 " This little room,
Where you have breakfasted and dined and supped,
And laughed and chatted in the days gone by,
Will be a lonely place when we are gone.
Those roses at the window, that were wont
To bloom so freely with the lady's care,

Already miss her touch.   That ivy-vine
Has grown a yard since it was tied, and needs
A training hand."

                    Rising with bitter tears
To flee his presence, he arose with me,
And wandered through the rooms.

                              "This casket here"—
I heard him say: "Suppose we loose the clasp.
These are her jewels—pretty gifts of yours.
There is a diamond: there a string of pearls.
That paly opal holds a mellowed fire
Which minds me of the mistress, whose bright soul
Glows through the lucent whiteness of her face
With lambent flicker.   These are legacies:
She will not wear them more.   Her taste and mine
Are one in this, that both of us love flowers.
Ay, she shall have them, too, some pleasant day,
When she goes forth with me!

                    "So? what is this?

Her wardrobe! Let the door be opened wide!
This musk, so blent with scent of violets,
Revives one. You remember when she wore
That lavender?—a very pretty silk!
Here is a *moire antique.* Ah! yes—I see!
You did not like her in it. 'Twas too old,
And too suggestive of the dowager.
There is your favorite—that glossy blue—
The sweet tint stolen from the skies of June—
But she is done with it. I wonder who
Will wear it, when your grief shall find a pause!
Your daughter—possibly? . . . You shiver, sir!
Is it the velvet? Like a pall, you think!
Well, close the door!

        "Those slippers on the rug:
The time will come when you will kiss their soles
For the dear life that pressed them. Their rosettes
Will be more redolent than roses then.
You did not know how much you loved your wife?
I thought so!

        "This way! Let us take our stand

Beside her bed.   Not quite so beautiful
To your fond eyes as when she was a bride,
Though still a lovely woman!   Seems it strange
That she is yours no longer?—that her hand
Is given to another—to the one
For whom she has been waiting all her life,
And ready all her life?   Your power is gone
To punish rivals.   There you stand and weep,
But dare not lift a finger, while with smiles
And kindly welcome she extends her hands
To greet her long-expected friend.   She knows
Where I will take her—to what city of God,
What palace there, and what companionship.
She knows what robes will drape her loveliness,
What flowers bedeck her hair, and rise and fall
Upon the pulses of her happy breast.
And you, poor man! with all your jealous pride,
Have learned that she would turn again to you,
And to your food and furniture of life,
With disappointment.

       "Ay, she pities you—

Loves you, indeed; but there is One she loves
With holier passion, and with more entire
And gladder self-surrender.   She will go—
You know that she will go—and go with joy;
And you begin to see how poor and mean,
When placed beside her joy, are all your gifts,
And all that you have won by them.

                              "Poor man!
Weeping again!   Well, if it comfort you,
Rain your salt tears upon her waxen hands,
And kiss them dry at leisure!   Press her lips,
Hot with the hectic!   Lay your cold, wet cheek
Against the burning scarlet of her own:
Only remember that she is not yours,
And that your paroxysms of grief and tears
Are painful to her."

                              Ah! to wait for death!
To see one's idol with the signature
Of the Destroyer stamped upon her brow,
And know that she is doomed, beyond all hope;

To watch her while she fades ; to see the form
That once was Beauty's own become a corpse
In all but breathing, and to meet her eyes
A hundred times a day—while the heart bleeds—
With smiles of smooth dissembling, and with words
Cheerful as morning, and to do all this
Through weeks and weary months, till one half longs
To see the spell dissolved, and feel the worst
That death can do: can there be misery
Sadder than this?

            My time I passed alone,
And at the bedside of my dying wife.
She talked of death as children talk of sleep,
When—a forgetful blank—it lies between
Their glad impatience and a holiday.
The morrow—ah! the morrow! That was name
For hope all realized, for work all done,
For pain all past, for life and strength renewed,
For fruitage of endeavor, for repose,
For heaven!

What would the morrow bring to me?
The morrow—ah! the morrow!   It was blank—
Nay, blank and black with gloom of clouds and night
Never before had I so realized
My helplessness.   I could not find relief
In love or labor.   I could only sit,
And gaze against a wall, without the power
To pierce or climb.   My pride of life was gone,
My spirit broken, and my strife with God
Was finished.   If I could not look before,
I dared not look above; and so, whene'er
I could forget the present, I went back
Upon the past.

One soft June day, my thoughts,
Touched by some song of bird, or glimpse of green,
Returned to life's bright morning, and the Junes
That flooded with their wealth of life and song
The valley of my birth.   Again I walked the meads,
Brilliant with beaded grass, and heard the shrill,
Sweet jargon of the meadow-birds.   Again
I trod the forest paths, in shade of trees

With foliage so tender that the sun
Shot through the soft, thin leaves its virid sheen,
As through the emerald waters of the sea.
The scarlet tanager—a flake of fire,
Blown from the tropic heats upon the breath
That brought the summer—caught upon a twig,
Or quenched its glow in some remote recess.
The springing ferns unfolded at my feet
Their tan-brown scrolls, the tiny star-flower shone
Among its leaves; the insects filled the air
With a monotonous, reedy resonance
Of whir and hum, and I sat down again
Upon a bank, to gather violets.

From dreams of retrospective joy I woke
At last, to the quick tinkle of a bell.
My wife had touched it. She had been asleep,
And, waking, called me to her side. The note,
Familiar as the murmur of her voice,
For the first time was strange. Another bell,
With other music, rang adown the years
That lay between me and the golden day

12

When, up the mountain-path, I followed far
The lamb that bore it.　All the scene came back
In a broad flash; and with it came the same
Strange apprehension of a mighty change—
A vague prevision of transition, born
Of what, I knew not; on what errand sent,
I could not guess.

　　　　　　　　　　I rose upon my feet,
Responsive to the summons, when I heard,
Repeated in the ear of memory,
The words my mother spoke to me that day:

" My Paul has climbed the noblest mountain-hight
" In all his little world. and gazed on scenes
" As beautiful as rest beneath the sun.
" I trust he will remember all his life
" That, to his best achievement, and the spot
" Closest to heaven his youthful feet have trod,
" He has been guided by a guileless lamb.
" It is an omen which his mother's heart
" Will treasure with her jewels.

                              Had her tongue
Been moved to prophecy?   Omen of what?—
Of a new hight of life to be achieved
By my lamb's leading?   Ay, it seemed like this!
An answer to a thousand prayers, up-breathed
By her whom I had lost, repeated long
By her whom I was losing?   Was it this?
Thus charged with premonition, when I stepped
Into the shaded room, my cheeks were pale,
And every nerve was quivering with the stress
Of uncontrolled emotion.   Ah! my lamb!
How white!   How innocent!   My lamb, my lamb!
Even the scarlet ribbon which adorned
The lambkin of my chase was at her throat,
Repeated in a bright geranium-flower!

"Loop up the curtains, love!   Let in the light!"
The words came strong and sweet, as if the life
From which they breathed were at its tidal flood.
"Oh! blessed light!" she added, as the sun
Flamed on the velvet roses of the floor,

And touched to life the pictures on the wall,
And smote the dusk with bars of amber.

                    "Paul!"

I turned to answer, and beheld a face
That glowed with a celestial fire like his
Who talked with God in Sinai.

                              "Paul," she said,
"I have been almost home. I may not tell,
For language cannot paint, what I have seen.
The veil was very thin, and I so near,
I caught the sheen of multitudes, and heard
Voices that called and answered from afar
Through spaces inconceivable, and songs
Whose harmonies responsive surged and sank
On the attenuate air, till all my soul
Was thrilled and filled with music, and I prayed
To be let loose, that I might cast myself
Upon the mighty tides, and give my life
To the supernal raptures. Ay, I prayed

That death might come, and give me my release
From this poor clay, and that I might be born
By its last travail into life."

                              "Dear wife," I said,
"You have been wildly dreaming, and your brain,
Quickened to strange vagaries by disease,
Has cheated you.   You must not talk like this:
'Twill harm you.   I will hold your hand awhile,
And you shall have repose."

                         She smiled and said,
While her eyes shone with an unearthly light:
"You are not wise, my dear, in things like these.
The vision was as real as yourself;
And it will not be long before I go
To mingle in the life that I have seen.
I know it, dearest, for she told me this."

"She told you this?" I said,—"Who told you this?
Did you hold converse with the multitude?"

"Not with the multitude," she answered me;
"But while I gazed upon the throng, and prayed
That death might loose me, there appeared a group
Of radiant ones behind the filmy veil
That hung between us, looking helplessly
Upon my struggle, but with eyes that beamed
With love ineffable.   I knew them too—
Knew all of them but one—and she the first,
And sweetest of them all.   Pure as the light,
And beautiful as morning, she advanced;
And, at her touch, the veil was parted wide,
While she passed through, and stood beside my bed.
She took my hand, she kissed my burning cheek,
And then, in words that calmed my spirit, said:

"Your prayer will soon be answered; but one prayer,
Breathed many years by you, and many years
By one you know not, must be answered first.
You must go back, though for a little time,
And reap the harvest of a life.   To him
Whom you and I have loved, say all your heart
Shall move your lips to speak, and he will hear.

The strength, the boldness, the persuasive power
Which you may need for this, shall all be yours;
For you shall have the ministry of those
Whom you have seen.   Speak as a dying wife
Has liberty to speak to him she leaves;
And tell him this—that he may know the voice
That gives you your commission—tell him this:
The lamb has slipped the leash by which his hand
Held her in thrall, and seeks the mountain-hight;
And he, if he reclaim her to his grasp,
Must follow where she leads, and kneel at last
Upon the summit by her side.   And more:
Give him my promise that if he do this,
He shall receive from that fair altitude
Such vision of the realm that lies around,
Cleft by the river of immortal life,
As shall so lift him from his selfishness,
And so enlarge his soul, that he shall stand
Redeemed from all unworthiness, and saved
To happiness and heaven."

Her words flowed forth

With the strong utterance, in truth, of one
Inspired from other worlds ; while pale and faint,
I drank her revelations.   Unbelief
Had given the lie to her abounding faith,
And held her vision figment of disease,
Until the message of my mother fell
Upon my ears.   Then overcome, I wept
With deep convulsions, rose and walked the room,
Wrung my clasped hands, and cried with choking voice,
"My mother ! O ! my mother !"

                              "Gently, love !
For she is with you," said my dying wife.
"Nay, all of them are with us.   This small room
Is now the gate of heaven ; and you must do
That which befits the presence and the place.
Come ! sit beside me ; for my time is short,
And I have much to say.   What will you do
When I am gone?   Will the old life of art
Content you?   Will you fill your waiting time
With the old dreams of fame and excellence?"

"Alas !" I answered, "I am done with life :

My life is dead; and though my hand has won
All it has striven to win, and all my heart
In its weak pride has prompted it to seek
Of love and honor ; though success is mine
In all my eager enterprise, I know
My life has been a failure.   I am left
Or shall be left, when you, my love, are gone,
Without resource—a hopeless, worthless man,
Longing to hide his shame and his despair
Within the grave."

                    "I thank thee, Lord!" she said :
"So many prayers are answered! . . . . You knew not
That I had asked for this.   You did not know
When you were striving with your feeble might
For the great prizes that beguiled your pride,
That at the hand of God I begged success.
Ay, Paul, I prayed that you might gather all
The good that you have won, and that, at last,
You might be brought to know the worthlessness
Of every selfish meed, and feel how weak—
How worse than helpless—is the highest man

Who lives within, and labors to, himself.
Not one of all the prizes you have gained
Contains the good that lies in your despair."

"Teach me," I said, "for I am ignorant;
Lead me, for I am blind.   Explain the past,
With all its errors.   Why am I so low,
And you so high?"

        She pressed my hand, and said:
" You have been hungry all your life for God,
And known it not.   You lavished first on me
Your heart's best love.   You poured its treasured wealth
At an unworthy shrine.   You made a God
Of poor mortality ; and when you learned
Your love was greater than the one you loved—
The one you worshiped—you invoked the aid
Of your imagination, to enrich
Your pampered idol, till at last you bowed
Before a creature of your thought.   You stole
From excellence divine the grace and good
That made me worshipful ; and even these

Palled on your heart at last, and ceased to yield
The inspiration that you craved. You pined,
You starved for something infinitely sweet;
And still you sought it blindly, wilfully
In your poor wife,—sought it, and found it not,
Through wasted years of life.

                         " And then you craved
An infinite return. You asked for more
Than I could give, although I gave you all
That woman can bestow on man. You knew
You held my constant love, unlimited
Save by the bounds of mortal tenderness;
And still you longed for more. Then sprang your scheme
For finding in the love of multitudes,
And in their praise, that which had failed in me.
You wrote for love and fame, and won them both
By manly striving—won and wore them long.
All good there is in love and praise of men,
You garnered in you life. On this reward
You lived, till you were sated, or until
You learned it bore no satisfying meed—

Learned that the love of many was not more
Than love of one. With all my love your own,
With love and praise of men, your famished soul
Craved infinite approval—craved a love
Beyond the love of woman and of man.

"Then with new hope, you apotheosized
Your cherished art, and sought for excellence
And for your own approval ; with what end,
Your helplessness informs me. You essayed
The revelation of the mighty forms
That dwell in the unrealized. You sought
To shape your best ideals, and to find
In the grand scheme your motive and reward.
All this blind reaching after excellence,
Was but the reaching of your soul for God.
Imagination could not touch the hight ;
And you were baffled. So, you failed to find
The God your spirit yearned for in your art,
And failed of self-approval.

                              " You have now

But one resource,—you are shut up to this:
You must bow down and worship God ; and give
Your heart to him, accept his love for you,
And feast your soul on excellence in him.
So, a new life shall open to your feet,
Strown richly with rewards ; and when your steps
Shall reach the river, I will wait for you
Upon the other shore, and we shall be
One in the life immortal as in this.
O ! Paul ! your time is now.   I cannot die
And leave you comfortless.   I cannot die
And enter on the pleasures that I know
Await me yonder, with the consciousness
That you are still unhappy."

                    All my life
Thus lay revealed in light which she had poured
Upon its track.   I learned where she had found
Her peaceful joy, her satisfying good,
And where, in my rebellious pride of heart,
Mine had been lost.   She, by an instinct sure,
Or by the grace of Heaven, had in her youth,

Though sorely chastened, given herself to God ;
And through a life of saintly purity —
A life of love to me and love to all —
Had feasted at the fountain of all love.
Had worshiped at the Excellence Divine,
And only waited for my last adieu
To take her crown.

      I sat like one struck dumb.
I knew not how to speak, or what to do.
She looked at me expectant; while a thrill
Of terror shot through all my frame.

         " Alas !"
She said, " I thought you would be ready now."

At this, the door was opened silently,
And our dear daughter stood within the room.
Alarmed at vision of the sudden change
That death had wrought upon her mother's face,
She hastened to her side, and kneeling there,
Bowed on her breast with tears and choking sobs,
Her heart too full for speech.

"Be silent, dear!"
The dying mother said, resting her hand
Upon her daughter's head. "Be silent, dear!
Your father kneels to pray. Make room for him,
That he may kneel beside you."

At her words,
I was endowed with apprehensions new;
And somewhere in my quickened consciousness,
I felt the presence of her heavenly friends,
And knew that there were spirits in the room.
I did not doubt, nor have I doubted since,
That there were loving witnesses of all
The scenes enacted round that hallowed bed.
Ay, and they spoke. Deep in the innermost
I heard the tender words, "O! kneel my son!—"
A sweet monition from my mother's lips.

"Kneel! kneel!" It was the echo of a throng.

"Kneel! kneel!" The gentle mandate reached my heart
From depths of lofty space. It was the voice
Of the Good Father.

From the curtain folds,
That rustled at the window, in the airs
That moved with conscious pulse to passing wings,
Came the same burden " Kneel!"

"Kneel! kneel!   O! kneel!"
In tones of earnest pleading, came from lips
Already pinched by death.

A hundred worlds,
Imposed upon my shoulders, had not bowed
And crushed me to my knees with surer power.
The hand that lay upon my daughter's head
Then passed to mine; but still my lips were dumb.

"Pray!" said the spirit of my mother.

"Pray!"
The word repeated, came from many lips.

"Pray!" said the voice of God within my soul;
While every whisper of the living air
Echoed the low command.

"Pray! pray! O! pray!"
My dying wife entreated, while swift tears
Slid to her pillow.

                Then the impulse came,
And I poured out like water all my heart.
"O! God!" I said, "be merciful to me
A reprobate!   I have blasphemed thy name,
Abused thy patient love, and held from thee
My heart and life ; and now, in my extreme
Of need and of despair, I come to thee.
O! cast me not away, for here, at last,
After a life of selfishness and sin,
I yield my will to thine, and pledge my soul—
All that I am, all I can ever be—
Supremely to thy service.   I renounce
All worldly aims, all selfish enterprise,
And dedicate the remnant of my power
To thee and those thou lovest.   Comfort me!
O! come and comfort me, for I despair!
Give me thy peace, for I am rent and tossed!
Feed me with love, else I shall die of want!

Behold! I empty out my worthlessness,
And beg thee to come in, and fill my soul
With thy rich presence.   I adore thy love;
I seek for thy approval; I bow down,
And worship thee, the Excellence Supreme.
I've tasted of the sweetest that the world
Can give to me; and human love and praise,
And all of excellence within the scope
Of my conception, and my power to reach
And realize in highest forms of art,
Have left me hungry, thirsty for thyself.
O! feed and fire me!   Fill and furnish me!
And if thou hast for me some humble task—
Some service for thyself, or for thy own—
Reveal it to thy sad, repentant child,
Or use him as thy willing instrument.
I ask it for the sake of Jesus Christ,
Henceforth my Master!

                      Multitudes, it seemed,
Responded with "Amen!" as if the word
Were caught from mortal lips by swooping choirs

Of spirits ministrant, and borne away
In sweet reverberations into space.

I raised my head at last, and met the eyes
Bright with the light of death, and with the dawn
Of opening heaven. The smile that overspread
The fading features was the peaceful smile
Of an immortal, — full of faith and love —
A satisfied, triumphant, shining smile,
Lit by the heavenly glory.

      " Paul," she said,
" My work is done ; but you will live and work
These many years.   Your life is just begun,
Too late, but well begun ; and you are mine,
Now and forevermore. . . . . Dear Lord ! my thanks
For this thy crowning blessing ! "

      Then she paused,
And raised her eyes in a seraphic trance,
And lifted her thin fingers, that were thrilled
With tremulous motion, like the slender spray

On which a throbbing song-bird clings, and pours
His sweet incontinence of ecstasy,
And then in broken whispers said to me:
"Do you not hear them?   They have caught the news;
And all the sky is ringing with their song
Of gladness and of welcome.   '*Paul is saved!*
Paul is redeemed and saved!' I hear them cry;
And myriad voices catch the new delight,
And carry the acclaim, till heaven itself
Sends back the happy echo: '*Paul is saved!*'"

She stretched her hands, and took me to her breast.
I kissed her, blessed her, spoke my last adieu,
And yielded place to her whom God had given
To be our child.   After a long embrace,
She whispered: "I am weary; let me sleep!"

She passed to peaceful slumber like a child,
The while attendant angels built the dream
On which she rode to heaven.   Not once again
She spoke to mortal ears, but slept and smiled,
And slept and smiled again, till daylight passed.

The night came down ; the long hours lapsed away ;
The city sounds grew fainter, till at last
We sat alone with silence and with death.
At the first blush of morning she looked up,
And spoke, but not to us : " I'm coming now !"

I sought the window, to relieve the pain
Of long suppressed emotion.   In the East,
Tinged with the golden dawn, the morning star
Was blazing in its glory, while beneath,
The slender moon, at its last rising, hung,
Paling and dying in the growing light,
And passing with that leading up to heaven.
My daughter stood beside her mother's bed,
But I had better vision of the scene
In the sweet symbol God had hung for me
Upon the sky.

            Swiftly the dawn advanced,
And higher rose, and still more faintly shone,
The star-led moon.   Then, as it faded out,
Quenched by prevailing day, I heard one sigh—

A sigh so charged with pathos of deep joy,
And peace ineffable, that memory
Can never lose the sound ; and all was past !

The peaceful summer-day that rose upon
This night of trial and this morn of grief,
Rose not with calmer light than that which dawned
Upon my spirit.   Chastened, bowed, subdued,
I kissed the rod that smote me, and exclaimed :
' The Lord hath given ; the Lord hath taken away ;
And blessed be his name ! "

                          Rebellion slept.
I grieved, and still I grieve ; but with a heart
At peace with God, and soft with sympathy
Toward all my sorrowing, struggling, sinful race.
My hope, that clung so fondly to the world
And the rewards of time, an anchor sure
Now grasps the Eternal Rock within the veil
Of troubled waters.   Storms may wrench and toss,
And tides may swing me, in their ebb and flow,
But I shall not be moved.

Once more! once more!
I shall behold her face, and clasp her hand!
Once more—forevermore!

So here I give
The gospel of her precious, Christian life.
I owe it to herself, and to the world.
Grateful for all her tender ministry
In life and death, I bring these leaves, entwined
With her own roses, dewy with my tears,
And lay them as the tribute of my love
Upon the grave that holds her sacred dust.

END OF KATHRINA.

Condensed Catalogue

OF THE PUBLICATIONS OF

CHARLES SCRIBNER & Co.,

654 BROADWAY,

NEW YORK.

JANUARY, 1868.

*** *The figures in the last column of this Catalogue refer to* CHARLES SCRIBNER & CO.'S *Descriptive Catalogue, copies of which will be sent to any address upon application.*

*** *Blanks in the column of prices, except in the case of School Text-Books, the prices of which may be learned from* CHARLES SCRIBNER & CO.'S *Educational Catalogue, indicate that the Works are either out of print or in press.*

*** *In this list the names of Books just published are given in* SMALL CAPITALS; *those issued during the year* 1867, *as well as new editions of Works previously produced, are indicated by italics.*

*** *The prices here given are for the regular style of binding in cloth.* Books *furnished in other styles, and their respective prices, may be learned from the Descriptive Catalogue.*

*** *Any of these Books will be sent post-paid to any address upon receipt of the price.*

	Volumes	Size.	Price.	Page
ADAMS, W., D.D.				
THANKSGIVING	I	12mo	$2 00	2
Three Gardens	I	12mo	2 00	I
AGASSIZ, PROF. LOUIS.				
Structure of Animal Life (The)	I	8vo	2 50	2
ALEXANDER, A., D.D.				
Moral Science	I	12mo	I 50	3
ALEXANDER, J. W., D.D.				
Alexander, Archibald, Life of, (Portrait)	I	12mo	2 00	3
Christian Faith and Practice (Discourses)	I	12mo	2 00	6
Consolation (Discourses)	I	12mo	2 00	5
Faith (Discourses)	I	12mo	2 00	6
Forty Years' Correspondence with a Friend	2	12mo	4 00	4
Preaching, Thoughts on	I	12mo	2 00	5

	Volumes.	Size.	Price.	Page.
ALEXANDER, J. A., D.D.				
Acts (Commentary)	2	12mo	$4 00	8
Isaiah " (complete)	2	8vo	6 50	7
" " (abridged)	2	12mo	4 00	8
Mark "	1	12mo	2 00	8
Matthew "	1	12mo	2 00	8
Psalms "	3	12mo	6 00	7
New Test. Literature and Ecc. Hist.	1	12mo	2 00	9
Sermons (with Portrait)	2	12mo	——	9
ALLSTON, WASHINGTON.				
Lectures and Poems	1	12mo	2 50	9
ANDREWS, REV. S. J.				
Life of Our Lord	1	post 8vo	3 00	10
ARMSTRONG, G. D., D.D.				
Works of	3	12mo ea.	1 25	11
BAUTAIN, PROF. A.				
Extempore Speaking	1	12mo	1 50	12
BEECHER, REV. H. W.				
PRAYERS FROM PLYMOUTH PULPIT	1	12mo	1 75	13
BOTTA, PROF.				
Dante as Poet, Patriot, Philosopher	1	crown 8vo	2 50	14
BRACE, CHARLES L.				
Hungary, with Experience of Austrian Police,	1	12mo	——	15
Home Life in Germany	1	12mo	——	14
Norse Folk	1	12mo	2 00	15
Races of Old World	1	post 8vo	2 50	15
Short Sermons for Newsboys	1	16mo	1 50	16
BUSHNELL, HORACE, D.D.				
Character of Jesus	1	18mo	1 00	19
Christ and his Salvation	1	12mo	2 00	19
Christian Nurture	1	12mo	2 00	18
Nature and the Supernatural	1	12mo	2 25	17
New Life, Sermons for	1	12mo	2 00	19
Vicarious Sacrifice, The	1	8vo	3 00	18
Work and Play	1	12mo	2 00	19
CHEEVER, G. B., D.D.				
Works of	3	12mo	——	20
CLARK, PROF. N. G.				
English Language, Elements of	1	12mo	1 25	21
COLLIER, J. PAYNE, F.S.A.				
Rarest Books in English Language	4	small 8vo	12 00	21
CONYBEARE, REV. W. J., and HOWSON, REV. J. S.				
St. Paul, Life and Epistles of (illustrated)	2	8vo	7 50	23

	Volumes.	Size.	Price.	Page.
TAYLOR, GEORGE.				
Indications of the Creator.	1	12mo	1 75	105
TENNEY, S., A.M.				
Natural History	1	crown 8vo	3 00	104
" " Library Edition . . .	1	large 8vo	4 00	104
" " for Schools	1	12mo	2 00	104
TIMOTHY TITCOMB.				
Complete Works of. See HOLLAND.	—	—	—	55–59
TRENCH, RT. REV. R. C.				
Epistles to Seven Churches, Commentary on	1	12mo	1 50	106
Studies in the Gospels	1	8vo	3 00	106
Glossary of English Words	1	12mo	1 50	107
Synonyms of New Testament (1st and 2d Series)	2	12mo ea.	1 25	107
TUCKERMAN, H. T.				
America and her Commentators . . .	1	crown 8vo	2 50	108
TULLIDGE, REV. H.				
Triumphs of the Bible	1	12mo	2 00	108
TUTHILL, MRS. L. C.				
Joy and Care. Book for Young Mothers .	1	16mo	1 00	109
VAN SANTVOORD, GEO.				
Lives of Chief Justices of U. S. . . .	1	8vo		109
WHITNEY, PROF. W. D.				
LANGUAGE, AND THE STUDY OF LANGUAGE	1	crown 8vo	2 50	110
WILLIS, N. P.				
Complete Works of				{ 111 / 112
WISE, CAPT. H. A.				
Works of	2	12mo ea.	1 75	112
WOOLSEY, PREST. T. D.				
International Law, Introduction to . .	1	8vo	2 50	113
WYLIE, S. B., D.D.				
McLeod, Alexander, Life of . . .	1	8vo	2 00	114
ZINCKE, F. BARHAM.				
Extemporary Preaching	1	12mo	1 50	114

ILLUSTRATED GIFT-BOOKS.

*** *In this list the prices of the respective works as bound in cloth, full gilt, are given. All of them, however, are furnished in Turkey morocco, and the prices of these editions may be learned by reference to the catalogue.*

	Price.	Page.		Price.	Page.
ÆSOP'S FABLES . . .	$18 00	117	FRED AND MARIA AND ME .	$1 50	121
Bitter-Sweet . . .	9 00	117	*Folk Songs*	15 00	115
Book of Rubies . . .	7 00	119	MY FARM OF EDGEWOOD .	10 00	121
Christian Armor . . .	15 00	120	Pilgrim's Progress . .	5 00	120
Cotter's Saturday Night .	5 00	119	QUEENS OF AMERICAN SOCIETY	6 00	118
FLORAL BELLES . .	25 00	116			

www.ingramcontent.com/pod-product-compliance
Lightning Source LLC
Chambersburg PA
CBHW020504270326
41926CB00008B/732